YOU GOT THIS!

*An Action Plan To Calm Fear, Anxiety,
Worry, And Stress*

LINDA BJORK

Printed in the United States of America
First Printing 2020
First Edition 2020

ISBN 9798643592846

Library of Congress Catalog Card Number: TXu002196541

10 9 8 7 6 5 4 3 2 1

Disclaimer:
This book is not designed for use as a medical reference to diagnose, treat, or prevent medical or mental health illnesses or trauma. If you have questions about the diagnosis, treatment, or prevention of a medical condition or mental illness, you should consult your personal physician or other mental health professional.

Cover design by Izabeladesign
For current information about all releases
from Linda Bjork, visit our website
lindabjorkauthor.com

YOU GOT THIS!

TABLE OF CONTENTS

1.

WELCOME, THREE EXAMPLES, AND INTRODUCTION

Welcome

You Got This! is a well-designed action plan that will empower you to calm fear, anxiety, worry, and stress!

Chronic fear, anxiety, worry, and stress can negatively affect our performance at work, our relationships, our happiness, and our well-being. They have been shown to cause numerous health problems including: anxiety disorders and panic attacks, depression, headaches, high blood pressure, heart disease, cardio-vascular problems, increased rapid heart-beat and heart palpitations, memory and concentration problems, problems with digestion, irritable bowel problems, upset stomach, ulcers, and acid reflux, trouble sleeping, weight gain, weakening of the immune system (making you more likely to have colds or other infections), and increase in blood sugar levels.

But there are ways to calm fear, anxiety, worry, and stress and I'll show you how. In this book we're going to discuss ways to decrease our stressors and increase our coping skills. I'll share tools to help you calm down and get back to the top of your game by broadening your vision and tapping into your own creative problem solving skills.

But that's not all. Skills are acquired by learning and practicing, so I'll guide you through a complete action plan of simple, consistent exercises that will alleviate fear and increase a sense of peace and control in your life.

Three examples

Everyone has experienced fear, anxiety, worry and/or stress during their life. The following personal stories illustrate a few of the many types of events that may trigger these emotions.

Near miss

My husband Lewis is a professional pilot. Flying is his passion. It is his identity. His father was a private pilot and flew a small private plane for business trips, so Lewis had the opportunity to begin experiencing flying from his infancy. He remembers first taking a turn at the controls at age five with his father as pilot in command in the left seat. He filled reams of paper with his childish sketches of airplanes. He built and flew model airplanes. He talked of planes and he dreamed of planes. As soon as he was old enough, he got a job to begin earning and saving for flight training. By age seventeen, the minimum legal age for obtaining a private pilot's license, he could proudly identify himself as a "pilot."

As an eighteen-year-old, with a year of flight experience under his belt and bursting with confidence, Lewis invited his friend Ron for an airplane ride. Although he had reasonable skill for such a young aviator, he was still a teenager, complete with teenage wisdom and teenage pride. Lewis wanted to be as impressive as possible, making a show about every slight technicality he could find with his hands unnecessarily flitting about the instrument panel in what he believed was an impressive display of aeronautical prowess. Eventually he glanced over at Ron fully expecting him to be in a rapturous state of awe, but his friend seemed equally unimpressed with the rented Cessna 172 and with Lewis' piloting skills. Rather than admiring Lewis at the controls, he seemed preoccupied with the view out the window. Disappointed, Lewis looked away secretly wishing for some aerobatic skills. Surely Ron would be impressed if he could show him that view from upside down.

Then, like thrusting a knife into Lewis' wounded pride, Ron commented that an airplane ride was not the sky-in-your-face wrestling match with death that Lewis had made it out to be. It was more like riding around in a car with a great view.

Lewis defended his beloved plane by pointing out that a car couldn't go this fast, referring to the airspeed indicator's blistering 105 knots, while secretly wishing they were flying in an F-16. As they were flying along the Wasatch Mountain Range, Lewis asked Ron if he would like to go up the canyon and inspect the snow conditions at Snowbird ski resort. Ron nodded. Surely this ought to be impressive, Lewis thought. Somewhere in the back of his mind, Lewis began to hear the admonitions of his father about the inherent danger of flying around these mountains, but he couldn't think of anything in particular, and he reasoned that he could always turn around. Besides they were almost at 6500 feet high, what could go wrong?

Snowbird ski resort was near the end of Little Cottonwood Canyon. The canyon terminates in a beautiful glacier-formed basin with a floor of 9000 feet, ringed on three sides with towering rocky cliffs. It didn't take long before Lewis realized his mistake. The mountain was rising more steeply than the plane could climb, and the canyon walls were too narrow for him to turn around. By choosing to turn up the canyon, he had put their lives in danger and he didn't see any way out. To make matters worse, they now penetrated the scattered veil of clouds. Lewis felt like a blindfolded prisoner facing the firing squad. He couldn't calm his rapid breathing, and felt little beads of sweat begin to break out on his forehead.

He focused as best as he could on simply flying the plane. He kept the wings level and maintained his heading. He understood the technical balance of the plane's limitations; by flying slower he could optimize the plane's rate of climb, but if he slowed too much, the plane would stall, meaning the wings would lose their power of lift, and the plane would plummet to the ground. His choices were limited to crashing forward, sideways, or straight down. He wondered how it would be. Would he have time to react, or would their bubble suddenly burst with an explosion of rock and charred aluminum? Would they make it to the end of the canyon, or scrape and tumble along the sides? He considered telling Ron, but thought maybe the morticians would prefer him looking peaceful. His lips began to quiver, and inside he began to pray.

Ron, on the other hand, was completely oblivious to their dire circumstances. He had no actual flight experience, but he had seen plenty of movies, and assumed that at any chosen moment, Lewis could simply turn the plane straight up and it would blast skyward with the power of a rocket, loop around and then take them back to the airport. Therefore, with eyes watching through the window, he commented on the intermittent views through the clouds. "Wow, it's really neat in these clouds!" And then, "Oh look, I can see the cliffs out this side of the plane!" Lewis' head jerked that way in time to see the cliffs passing eerily off the right wing tip and banked slightly left until the cliffs faded away in a cloudy gloom.

"We're dead," Lewis thought as he watched the altimeter just passing 8000 feet; breaks in the clouds were less frequent, and he had no idea exactly where they were. The cliffs to either side were invisible, and the boxed end of the canyon waited somewhere ahead.

Lewis continued to fly the plane, trying to hold that razor thin balance of flying as slowly, and climbing as steeply as he could without stalling the plane. When he heard the stall horn blare the warning of an impending stall, he had no choice but to slightly lower the nose of the plane. He knew it would be any minute now.

Then Ron commented that he saw skiers below. Lewis looked out and noticed the wires of the Snowbird aerial tram go by. They were close. They had reached the ski resort which signified that they were near the end of the canyon. That meant that cliffs were now in front of them as well as to the sides, and they could no longer go forward. "This is it," Lewis thought. He was in agony waiting to be hit, flinching at the thoughts of crashing into the cold granite rock. He banked hard left into the clouds. It very well might mean dying now, but he decided he'd rather risk hitting the side of the canyon trying to escape, than continuing forward into what he knew was certain death. No more waiting. It's over. He could feel the unseen canyon walls rushing the airplane as he blindly turned toward the invisible granite cliff. He made no attempt to maintain altitude. "Just make it quick," he thought.

To his utter surprise and relief, there was no crashing impact. The airplane simply turned around and descended out of the cloud layer. He did not understand until years later that by slowing the plane to 59 knots in a dismal effort to climb, it also meant that the plane could turn much tighter than it could if it was going faster. And by waiting until he reached the basin, the canyon walls were just wide enough for a miraculous escape. Lewis could have cried. Ron on the other hand, completely oblivious to their phenomenal good luck, continued to comment on the beautiful view.

The mouth of the canyon, now ahead of them, gleamed with sunlight splashing behind the breaks in the overcast sky. They poured out of the canyon and headed across the valley to the Municipal Airport. Lewis didn't want to fly anymore. He wanted to be on the ground. He wanted to stop shaking.

They landed and taxied to their parking spot. Since Lewis hadn't told Ron about their brush with death and his own stupidity that had placed them in this situation, he thought he could simply pretend that this was all in a day's work. No biggie, it was just a normal flight; but as he stepped outside the plane, his knees buckled and he collapsed like a soggy towel on the left main gear.

Ron, completely surprised, said, "Are you okay?"

Dreaded phone calls

When I was in my early 20's, I was serving as the secretary in a women's organization for my church. Part of my duties included calling people and making appointments so that the presidency, including myself, could visit with them to get to know and befriend them, and to ascertain needs, and see how we could offer help and support. I didn't know most of the people on this long list of names, and the idea of calling these strangers filled me with anxiety. I didn't know what to say. I didn't know how they would feel about my request to be visited by strangers. I was terrified of rejection. Everything about those phone calls filled me with dread, worry, and anxiety.

We did our weekly visits each Tuesday, and although the visits were scary for me, at least I had someone with me so I wasn't alone. If I didn't know what to say, certainly my companion would know the right words, but I carried the weight of responsibility for those phone calls by myself.

Each Tuesday night when we completed our visits, I came home with my heart and mind filled with dread that I had to make more phone calls to set up appointments for the following week. I worried about it on Wednesday. I worried about it on Thursday. I worried about it on Friday. I worried about it on Saturday, and by then it was getting worse because, of course, I hadn't actually called anybody and the deadline was approaching.

I worried about it on Sunday and finally pulled out my list of names. Fear and anxiety filled my heart as I called the first person. More often than not, no one answered, or if someone was home she rejected my request whether for scheduling conflicts or simply not being interested. Then I had to go through the process all over again, until I either succeeded in getting two appointments, or I gave up in frustration and failure. If that was the case, then I tried again on Monday. On Tuesday, we did our visits. Sometimes we had a nice visit, sometimes we had an awkward visit, and sometimes they stood us up and weren't home; but either way when the evening was over the process started all over again.

Granola days

My husband was training and preparing for his dream job as a professional pilot. The process is lengthy, intensive, and expensive. We had only been married a few years and I had recently quit my job so I could be home to care for our new baby. That change in employment status cut our income by about two thirds. Lewis was working as a flight instructor and the pay was dismal. Depending on his student workload, he brought home anywhere from $400-$800 each month. This was in the early 1990's so you'd have to account for inflation, but it was a pitifully small amount. We barely had enough to pay our rent, and on the good months we could also pay our utilities and gas for the car. There was no money for food or diapers, and there was no money for the additional training, flight time, and ratings that Lewis needed in order to meet the minimum requirements to be hired by the airlines. We were stuck in a place where merely surviving was a challenge, and progress seemed impossible.

My parents had given us some basic food staples as their gift to us the previous Christmas. Because of their generosity, we had some wheat, rolled oats, sugar, salt, and oil in our pantry. When we ran out of food in the fridge, I looked over these items and wondered what to do with them. I didn't have a clue what to do with the wheat. I didn't have a wheat grinder or grain mill to make it into flour.

I looked at the rolled oats. I knew how to make oatmeal, but I had grown up eating oatmeal, or "mush" as we called it, every day of my life, and I hated it every day of my life. My mother made either oatmeal or cracked wheat mush each morning and dished it into bowls. Each day I would rush to the table first so I could choose the smallest bowl. I vowed that when I was an adult and living on my own, I would never eat mush again. So even though our options were severely limited, I just couldn't bring myself to make oatmeal mush. I had recently learned how to make granola. So with the rolled oats, sugar, salt, oil, and a few additional ingredients that I borrowed from my mother, I made granola. Each day for months we had granola for breakfast, we had granola for lunch, and we had granola for dinner. It was all we had to eat. Today we call that time the "granola days."

I took a small job cleaning for an elderly couple a few hours a week so I could earn enough money for diapers and milk. It was one of the few options where I could take my infant son with me.

I was stressed, discouraged, and worried about having enough money to pay the bills. If we ever had an extra nickel, it had to be saved to pay for Lewis' training so he could eventually get a better paying job.

One day I learned some news from one of my neighbors that was the straw that broke the camel's back. She was a young expectant mother. At age fourteen she had moved in with her boyfriend, and now at age seventeen she was expecting their second child. She was complaining about her financial woes. They were receiving assistance from the government, help with housing, WIC, and so on. She said it was so hard to make ends meet when they only received $700 cash each month plus food. As she continued to expound on her distress, I realized that between the cash, food, and other benefits, they were bringing in about three times the resources that we were living off of.

Discouragement and depression overwhelmed me. My husband and I were both college graduates, and yet we were significantly worse off financially than a teenage mother on welfare. We weren't receiving any government assistance. We weren't receiving any assistance from our church or our families either. Neither set of our parents were wealthy, and we didn't want to bother them with our problems anyway. We actually hadn't told anyone about our extreme poverty. We were too embarrassed and ashamed. Besides that, we wanted to be able to do it by ourselves. The whole situation was demoralizing and humiliating. We were barely hanging on, and then our landlady informed us that she was raising the rent...

Fear comes in different intensities

Fear, anxiety, worry, and panic are emotions that most people are familiar with to some degree or another. While slightly different, each of these emotions are related and connected by the presence of fear.

Fear is an unpleasant emotion caused by the belief that someone or something is dangerous, likely to cause pain, or a threat.[1] Panic is an intense feeling of overpowering, extreme anxiety or terror while anxiety is an unpleasant, but vague sense of apprehension.[2]

Worry has a couple of definitions that may seem unrelated at first, but they are all connected.[3] First of all, worry means a state of anxiety and uncertainty over actual or potential problems. It implies concern mixed with fear. Worry can also mean to tear at, gnaw on, pull at, or fiddle with continually. A dog can worry a bone by continually gnawing at it. You can worry the knot at the end of a rope by continually fiddling with it and perhaps fraying it. It has to do with the idea of touching or disturbing something repeatedly. Worry is not a fleeting emotion, it tends to be nagging, persistent, and incessant. Some synonyms for worry include: to annoy, plague, pester, or torment.

Any of these forms of fear can cause stress. Stress is a state of mental or emotional strain or tension resulting from adverse or very demanding circumstances.[4]

Different causes of fear

Fear arises with the threat of harm, either physical, emotional, or psychological, and it can come from either real or imagined circumstances. These unpleasant emotions can arise from an imminent physical threat, like Lewis' experience flying up the canyon, or they may arise from a perceived emotional and mental threat like my assignment to call strangers on the phone. Work and financial concerns are some of the most common stressors that cause worry and anxiety.

Everyday life gives many opportunities to experience fear, anxiety, worry, stress, or even panic. The purpose of this book is to share coping skills to effectively deal with these challenges. As we learn to calm and manage those feelings and emotions, it increases our mental, emotional, and physical wellbeing, and improves our quality of life.

Neither good, nor bad, it just is

Emotions by themselves are neither good nor bad, instead they are either helpful or hurtful depending on intensity, duration, and circumstances.[5] Fear, anxiety and worry are psychological and physiological responses to danger and can be a central part of our harm avoidance system.[6] In other words, they are intended to keep us safe. However, if they get out of hand, they may interfere with our physical, mental, and emotional well-being. They can harm our health, performance, relationships, and happiness.

The positives

All emotions can have a positive aspect. Fear, anxiety, worry, and stress can activate the sympathetic nervous system often called the "fight or flight" response.[7] Activating the fight or flight system can help increase the physiological response known as arousal (not to be confused with sexual arousal). Arousal is the physiological and psychological state of being awoken, or of sense organs stimulated to a point of perception.[8] In other words, it means we're awake and alert. It increases heart rate and blood pressure, and causes a condition of sensory alertness, mobility, and readiness to respond. This higher state of arousal means we're ready to fight or run away as necessary, and it helps keep us safe.

In addition to protecting our wellbeing, a slight increase of arousal caused by fear, anxiety, worry, or stress can actually improve our performance. Increased arousal caused by feelings of stress when you're taking an important exam can help you focus on the test and remember the information that you studied. Likewise, when an athlete is poised to make an important move, like a basketball player shooting a free throw, an increased level of arousal can help him make the shot. Our bodies and minds perform better with a little bit of excitement or stress. However, this is true only up to an optimal point of arousal. If we feel too much stress or anxiety, then the level of performance drops, sometimes dramatically.[9] Too much test anxiety can impair your ability to concentrate and makes it more difficult to remember the correct answers, and if a basketball player gets too stressed out, he may choke and miss the shot.

Yerkes-Dodson Law

In psychology, this relationship between arousal levels and performance is known as the Yerkes-Dodson Law.[10] The Law was first described in 1908 by psychologists Robert Yerkes[11] and John Dillingham Dodson.[12] Through a series of experiments, they discovered that mild electrical shocks could be used to motivate rats to complete a maze, but when the shocks became too strong, the rats would scurry around in random directions trying to escape.

Their experiments suggest that there is a relationship between performance and arousal. Increased arousal can help improve performance, but only up to a certain point. At the point when arousal becomes excessive, performance diminishes.[13]

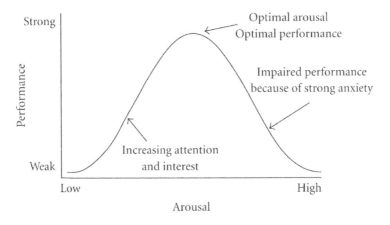

Lessons from Yerkes-Dodson curve

Fear, anxiety, worry, and stress are often considered "negative" emotions, but they are actually a part of a beautifully orchestrated design to benefit us by increasing our performance and keeping us safe. They are not our enemy and we don't need to eliminate them entirely or pretend that we don't have these emotions. Remember that according to the Yerkes-Dodson curve, a little bit of arousal caused by fear, anxiety, worry, or stress can actually improve our performance efficiency. If we have low arousal, we don't care and we don't perform very well, but with a moderate level of stress we actually increase our level of performance. We are energized to face whatever challenge is ahead.

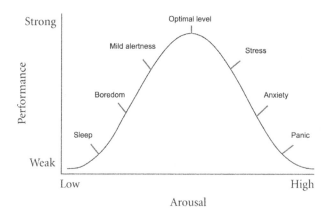

Anxiety disorders

However, high levels of stress and anxiety decrease performance because we become overwhelmed. The arousal caused by stress and anxiety no longer gives a little boost to help overcome challenges, instead they actually compound the problem by making it worse. Most people are aware of the negative consequences of stress and anxiety and its toll on society and on individuals. Anxiety disorders are the most common mental illness in the U.S., affecting 40 million adults in the United States age 18 and older, or 18.1% of the population every year.[14] That means that more than one out of every six people suffer from some type of anxiety disorder. Treating anxiety can be expensive; the average annual medical cost for individuals diagnosed with any anxiety disorder was estimated at $6,475 in 2005.[15]

Furthermore, it's not uncommon for someone with an anxiety disorder to also suffer from depression or vice versa. Nearly one-half of those diagnosed with depression are also diagnosed with an anxiety disorder.[16] Some experts believe that depression is caused by a feeling that you are unable to solve your problems. Therefore, learning how to cope with fear, anxiety, worry, and stress in a healthy manner is an excellent way to prevent depression from creeping in. We want to be able to calm and manage these emotions so that they can benefit us rather than harming us.

The autonomic nervous system

Understanding a little about the autonomic nervous system helps in understanding how the results of our emotions can be either helpful or hurtful. Our bodies have an autonomic nervous system which regulates bodily functions such as heart rate, digestion, respiratory rate, pupillary response, etc. The autonomic nervous system has separate branches. One is called the sympathetic nervous system, and is often called the "fight or flight" system. Another branch is called the parasympathetic nervous system, which is often called the "rest and digest" system.[17]

Parasympathetic (rest and digest)		Sympathetic (fight or flight)
	Eyes	
Constricts pupils		Dilates pupils
	Mouth	Inhibits salivation
Stimulates salivation		
	Heart	Accelerates heart rate
Slows heart rate		
Slower breathing	Lungs	Rapid breathing
Stimulates the activity of the digestive organs, pancreas and gall bladder	Stomach, digestive system	Inhibits the activity of the digestive organs, pancreas and gall bladder
		Conversion of glycogen to glucose raises blood sugar levels
Stimulates the release of bile	Liver	Stimulates the production of adrenaline and cortisol
	Bladder	
Contracts bladder		Relaxes bladder

Turning systems "on and off"

In many cases, both of these systems have opposite actions where one system activates a physiological response, and the other inhibits it. In other words, our bodies are designed to naturally take care of things like our digestion and immune system to keep us nourished and healthy; but during times of an emergency, the body puts those things on hold in order to direct energy into more important things like the ability to run away from danger right now.

Our bodies produce a stress hormone called cortisol, which is like a built-in alarm. It works with certain parts of your brain to control your mood, motivation, and fear. It accelerates heartbeat, increases blood sugar, and alters other body systems to prepare your body to respond to the danger. When your body is on high alert, cortisol can alter or shut down functions that get in the way. These might include your digestive or reproductive systems, your immune system, or even your growth processes.

After the danger has passed, then your cortisol level should calm down and your heart, blood pressure, and other body systems will get back to normal. This is a wonderful, natural, and automatic process designed to help keep us safe, and enable us to quickly respond to danger.

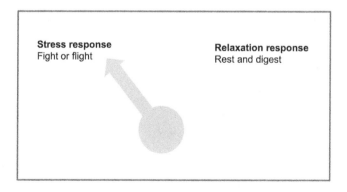

Stress response
Fight or flight

Relaxation response
Rest and digest

Chronic worry, anxiety, and stress

However, this "fight or flight" system is only intended to be in use for short periods of time; and if we keep our bodies constantly in the "fight or flight" response with worry and stress, it can negatively affect virtually every organ system in the body. According to the National Institutes of Health (NIH) prolonged stress has been shown to cause numerous health problems including:[18]

- Anxiety and depression
- Headaches
- Heart disease
- Memory and concentration problems
- Problems with digestion
- Trouble sleeping
- Weight gain
- Weakening of the immune system, making you more likely to have colds or other infections
- High blood pressure
- Upset stomach, ulcers and acid reflux
- Increased rapid heart beat and heart palpitations
- Panic attacks
- Cardio-vascular problems
- Increase in blood sugar levels
- Irritable bowel problems
- Backaches

- Tension headaches or migraines

- Chronic fatigue syndrome

- Respiratory problems and heavy breathing

- Worsening of skin conditions, such as eczema

This short list includes many of the physical problems that can arise from chronic fear, anxiety, worry, and stress, but there are also many social, mental, and emotional problems as well. Chronic fear, anxiety, worry, and/or stress can negatively affect our performance at work. It can negatively affect our relationships. It can negatively affect our happiness and well-being. When we're on the wrong side of that Yerkes-Dodson curve, our performance in every area diminishes.

Stressors and coping skills

A stressor is an activity, event, or other stimulus that causes stress. Stressors are those things that cause fear, anxiety, worry, stress, or panic in our lives. Coping refers to our response to those stressors. It relates to how we deal with and attempt to overcome problems and difficulties.

If we graph our stressors and our coping skills, we get a pretty good idea of our state of being. If our stressors are low and our coping skills are high, then we are at peace. If our stressors are high and coping skills are also high, it might be challenging, but are typically able to overcome any obstacles. However, if we find that the stressors are high, and our coping skills are low, then our feelings of stress are high, and we feel overwhelmed and unable to cope.

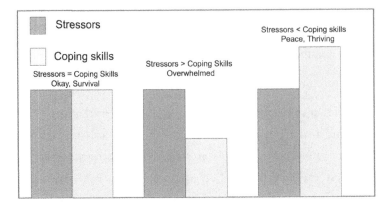

Expertise and somatic quieting

Our coping skills can typically be broken down into two areas of focus. The first is our expertise, in other words it is our level of skill, ability, confidence, and resources to do whatever task is before us. For example, a five-year-old may be overwhelmed by the task of adding six plus seven, but to a ten-year-old, that task is extremely simple. Likewise, for a fifteen or sixteen-year-old, the multidimensional skills necessary to drive a car may seem overwhelming, but an adult may find that same task relaxing, since it requires very little effort. This is true every time we learn a new skill. As our expertise level increases, the task becomes easier, and we're able to cope with the demands.

The relaxation response

Another aspect of coping skills is called somatic quieting.[19] Somatic quieting turns on the relaxation response in the body. The relaxation response is essentially the opposite reaction to the stress response. It is a process of turning the "rest and digest" system back on. This releases chemicals and brain signals to make your muscles and organs slow down, and increases blood flow to the brain.

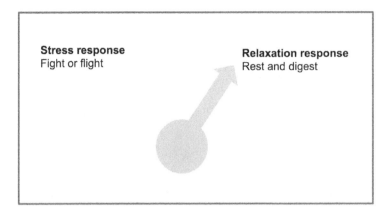

Stress response
Fight or flight

Relaxation response
Rest and digest

The term "relaxation response" was coined by Dr. Herbert Benson, an American medical doctor, cardiologist, author, and a founder of mind/body medicine.[20] His book, *The Relaxation Response*, describes the scientific benefits of relaxation and shows how it can be an effective treatment for a wide range of stress related disorders. The relaxation response counteracts the physiological effects of stress and the fight or flight response. His research conducted in the 1960s and 1970s helped demystify meditation, and brought it to the mainstream by demonstrating how meditation promotes better health, lower stress levels, increased wellbeing, and reduced blood pressure levels.

More benefits of the relaxation response

When our bodies and minds are in a constant state of fight or flight, it narrows our focus and gives us a sort of "tunnel vision." If we can get out of that fight or flight mentality and turn on the relaxation response, even for a few moments each day, it gives our body and our mind a break. It broadens our focus, and we are able to find new and creative ways to solve our problems. You are stronger than you think and smarter than you think. The answers to your problems are most likely already inside of you, you just need a way to tap into that greatness, and set it free. Therefore, these two separate aspects of coping skills, expertise and somatic quieting, are interrelated. Calming down and turning on the relaxation response helps us get back to the top of our game by broadening our vision and tapping into our own creative problem solving skills.

2.

COMMITMENT, INTENTION, AND WHAT TO EXPECT

Action plan

In this book we're going to discuss ways to decrease our stressors as well as ways to increase our coping skills. I'll share cognitive behavioral therapy (CBT)[21] tools that have been scientifically proven to be effective in lowering fear, anxiety, worry, and stress. We're going to learn somatic quieting skills, and how to broaden our vision to find answers to our problems.

But that's not all. Skills are acquired by learning and practicing, so we're not just going to talk about it. Positive changes require action, so I'll guide you through a series of simple, consistent actions that will alleviate fear and increase a sense of peace and control in your life.

I have created a simple schedule to guide you through the next thirty days. You may find that you need more than thirty days to complete the exercises in this book and that's perfectly okay. You may want to spend several days, or maybe even weeks or months, practicing and building particular skills that will be most beneficial to you. You may need to take longer breaks before delving into a new technique and that's okay too.

I know that your plate is already full, but don't worry, these won't take a lot of time. Everything in this book is designed to ease your burdens, not add to them. And I will explain what to do, and why we're doing it each step along the way.

The schedule for each day includes a brief morning routine to get the day started off right, a daily action step to acquire and practice skills, and finally a short evening routine to help you relax and enjoy better quality sleep.

Charts for each day are included in the appendix. A daily schedule looks something like this:

Morning routine

This should take about 15 minutes and includes three parts: nourishing the body, empowering, and building feelings of peace and safety. First we will do one simple thing to nourish the body. Three suggested methods are to take a good quality vitamin supplement with B-complex vitamins, or a green smoothie, or wheatgrass. The second step is about empowering and consists of two short exercises that consists of listening to music while spending 2 minutes focusing on an "I am" poster and then repeating a set of positive affirmations three times. The final step of the morning routine is to build feelings of peace and safety by either creating a virtual shield or doing a loving-kindness meditation.

Daily action step

This should take about 30 minutes. These will change each day, but I'll explain what to do and why to do it each step of the way

Evening routine

This should take about 15 minutes and includes an empowering exercise, like the morning routine, as well as somatic quieting through progressive relaxation.

Intention and commitment

My intention is to provide an effective action plan to help you relieve fear, anxiety, worry, and stress while increasing feelings of peace and well-being. I intend to share tools that will help you unlock the answers that are already inside of you, so that you will be better able to find solutions to your own problems.

However, my intention alone is not sufficient. We're going to turn to the expert for answers. Not *an* expert, *the* expert. You are the expert on you. You know your strengths. You know your weaknesses. You know your problems. You know your history. The answers to many of your challenges are actually already inside of you; and I'm going to help you find them through a series of small consistent steps that will help foster healing, alleviate fear, anxiety, worry, and stress, and allow the answers to begin to flow through you. But in order for this to be successful, my intentions need to be combined with *your* intention and *your* commitment.

Will you commit with me to work on improving your mental and emotional well-being for the next 30 days, and to follow the steps as outlined? A growing body of research shows that a person's mindset, intentions, and commitment level can measurably affect levels of success.[22, 23]

Please repeat the following intention.

My intention is to be at peace with myself, with others, and with my life circumstances and to experience joy and delight in each day. My intent is to willingly let go of any unnecessary fear, anxiety, worry, and stress, and to allow peace and feelings of safety to flow into my heart and mind. My intent is to gain confidence in my power and ability to handle my challenges. My intent is to open my eyes, my mind, and my heart to find solutions to my problems, and I'm delighted that it is easier than I ever thought possible. Therefore, I, _____, commit to follow the outlined steps for the next thirty days.

Thank you.

3.

OVERCOMING OBSTACLES AND EMOTIONAL FIRST AID KIT

Emotional walls

It is important to understand some challenges that are likely to arise when you attempt to move from a place of fear, anxiety, worry, and stress to a place of general peace and tranquility. These challenges come from two basic sources, and either one of them may make things worse before they get better, and they may make you want to quit and give up; but being properly informed empowers us to keep going and experience healing, peace, and growth in spite of obstacles in our path.

The reticular activating system

To understand why we hit emotional walls, it's helpful to understand a little about the normal function of the brain. There is a network of neurons located in the brain stem called the reticular activating system or (RAS)[24] which is the gateway into the brain. All of the sensory information that we encounter, first enters through the RAS which determines where to send it. The reticular activating system acts as a filter so we don't become overwhelmed by an overload of information. It is like a gatekeeper that chooses what information passes between the subconscious and conscious mind.

The job of the RAS is very important because it is estimated that the human brain takes in 11 million bits of information every second, but on average we're only consciously aware of 40 bits of information.[25] So when I say that the RAS filters information, I'm not talking about filtering out a little bit of information, I'm talking about a major filtering process. It is the job of the RAS to decide what is important and what can be safely ignored. When the RAS is deficient, such as in cases of autism, ADD, and ADHD, too much information is allowed into the conscious mind, and it causes a sensory overload and a difficulty in concentration and ability to focus. So the job of the RAS is very important to our safety, comfort, and functionality.

However, the next question is, *how* does the RAS decide which information is important? It makes those decisions based on automatic programming that you and I created without even being aware of it.[26] It is done on a subconscious level and is influenced by what we focus on. If we spend a lot of time focusing on a particular thing, then the automatic subconscious programming of the RAS assumes that information must be important.

That's why when you're trying to buy a new car and have been researching a particular make and model, all of the sudden you start to notice that car everywhere. The truth is that the cars were there all along, but the RAS considered that information to be something that was safe to ignore. However, now that you're focusing on it, the RAS figures that it must be important so it points them out for you.

The automatic subconscious programming of the RAS causes some problems when we're dealing with mental and emotional issues such as fear, anxiety, worry or stress. A person who is struggling with fear based emotions often has thoughts like, "I'm not safe. I'm in danger. The people I care about are in danger. I'm not strong enough. I'm overwhelmed. I can't do this. I can't handle this." And so on.

Because these are the predominant thought patterns, the RAS uses this as the basis for determining what is important. Since there is limited space for conscious awareness, anything that *doesn't* support those negative feelings are filtered out, and the only information that enters the conscious are those things that support those feelings of fear. That means that your brain is actively seeking for proof to validate these fearful beliefs. Your mind becomes hypersensitive to any possible threat, either real or imagined, present or future. Your brain also tunes in to any evidence that suggests that you're weak and can't handle your problems. This strengthens and builds on the problem by continually adding "evidence" that the feelings of fear and your own inadequacy are valid, and the situation becomes progressively worse.

Furthermore, if we make a conscious effort to say or do something that is contrary to the current subconscious programming, the brain considers this a dangerous threat and sends out a warning that in order to be safe, you need to go back. This makes change difficult, because if a person tries to let go of fear, anxiety, worry, and stress and actively seeks for evidence and feelings of safety and peace; those things don't match the current subconscious programming, and the warning system is activated.

Warning systems and first aid kits

When that warning hits, it feels like running into an impenetrable wall, and people naturally give up.[27] When I was going through this process, I hit that wall immediately and I wanted to give up on day one. It's difficult to adequately describe, but it literally felt like I was going to die. I felt all the emotional and physiological symptoms as if my life was being threatened, and my subconscious warned me that the only safe option was to go back. It was awful. Indescribably awful.

Fortunately, I had been warned that this would happen so I knew what to do. To get through that wall I used one of the tools in my emotional first aid kit.[28] An emotional first aid kit is a list of simple tools or actions that cause an immediate, although temporary, positive effect; like singing for example, and that's what I did. I cranked up one of Shakira's songs, called *Try Anything* from the movie Zootopia, and sang along.

Singing it through once wasn't enough, I had to repeat it three times before the feelings of panic that my life was in mortal danger subsided, and I knew I would survive.

The remedy is surprisingly simple, but it takes some courage to follow through. After all, it seems rather counter intuitive. Think about it. If you're watching a movie and a monster is chasing somebody, they respond by running away or hiding. They don't jump out and sing a song, because if they sing a song then the monster will find them and eat them; but if they run away or hide then there's a chance of survival. Turning to the tools in the first aid kit, rather than curling up in a ball on your bed, takes some courage and trust. After some practice and personal experience, you will find that the tools work and it won't be so scary to use them to get out of a tight spot. Keep a list of emotional tools handy, that work best for you, to use as an emotional first aid kit to work through those walls that try to obstruct progress.

If we can push through these walls and keep going, then our thoughts and feelings slowly change, and the RAS naturally adjusts its programming to allow positive, peaceful, hopeful input without fighting or outright rejecting it. So this fight with our subconscious is temporary during a transition period; but it's also inevitable, and this causes many people to give up because they don't understand what's happening. All they know is that there is a warning voice in their head that they're not safe, and so they quit and retreat.

But now you understand what is happening, why it's happening, and what to do about it, and that makes all the difference. When you know what to do, you can work through the rough spots to reach the peace, happiness, and healing available on the other side.

Mere exposure effect

There is another explanation for the emotional walls that attempt to block our path when we try to make any change in the way we respond to stressors. You may have heard the idea that if you hear something enough times you begin to believe it, and research shows that is absolutely true. We are more likely to believe things that we hear over and over again, just because we heard it over and over again, and it doesn't matter if it's true or not. We believe things because they are familiar. Scientists call this phenomenon the "mere exposure effect" and it's baffling because it has nothing to do with truth, reason, or logic.[29] This is another reason why it's so dangerous to have circulating thoughts and statements like, "I'm not safe.

I can't handle it. I'm not good enough, etc." If you repeat those thoughts and those statements often enough, you begin to believe them, even when they're not true. Furthermore, a child who has been told over and over again that they can't do something, or that they're stupid, or worthless, or not safe, or not good enough, will accept these familiar sayings as true.

The flip side of the coin is that once we believe something, whether or not it is true, our subconscious will fight to protect those beliefs by rejecting anything that is unfamiliar or contradicts what we already believe.[30] Sadly, that means that the child who has grown up with the belief that they're stupid, or worthless, or not safe, or not good enough, will then fight to defend and support those beliefs their whole life. That is, unless they go through the conscious effort to change those beliefs.

When feelings of fear, anxiety, worry, and stress are repeated over and over, they become familiar, and we believe them to be the only possible truth. It may seem ironic, but a person may subconsciously believe that feelings of fear, anxiety, worry, and stress are more "safe" than feelings of peace, serenity, calmness, and contentment, because those feelings are unfamiliar and therefore "dangerous." People often subconsciously fight to hold onto those fearful beliefs. They reject thoughts about happiness, positivity, hopefulness, confidence, relaxation, success, or peace because they contradict what their minds already believe to be true.

These two sources, the reticular activating system and the mere exposure effect, make it difficult to find peace when you're stuck in a pattern of fear. However, there is a difference between difficult and impossible.

You can do this. I'll freely admit that it's hard, but it's oh so worth it. Scientific research shows that if you're persistent, then those same principles of repetition that create familiarity can also change the way you think and the way you feel. But don't give up halfway or it will make it harder.[31] If you give up, the *walls* become stronger; but if you keep going, then *you* become stronger. Mental and emotional healing takes time and effort. It's not an immediate change like flipping on a light switch; it's more like the gradual change of watching a sunrise.

Remember, when you understand what is happening, why it's happening, and what to do about it, you can work through the rough spots to reach the peace, happiness, and healing available on the other side.

Both of these obstacles are temporary, if you don't give up, that is. In fact, both of these obstacles turn into allies once you get through that transition phase. If you hear and say over and over again that you're safe, capable, and peaceful then those words and those feelings will become familiar, and your mind will believe in those concepts. If the focus of the reticular activating system is safety, confidence, and peace, then your mind will show you all the reasons why you are safe and capable. It will highlight reasons to feel grateful, satisfied, joyful, and peaceful. The mere exposure effect can help you believe in the ideas of safety and peace, and then the RAS will gather evidence that those ideas are valid. They will work for you instead of against you.

Emotional first aid kit

The following section is a list of tools to use as an emotional first aid kit. Remember that an emotional first aid kit is just a list of tools that can provide an immediate, although temporary, positive effect. Use these anytime you hit an emotional wall, feel overwhelmed, or you just need a quick boost. Stick with me. You got this. You can knock those walls over, and turn them into stairs that will take you to a higher, happier plane.

Sing a song 3X

The first tool I'm going to share is to sing a song, because that's the first tool that got me through a rough spot. I felt threatened and it was like an impenetrable wall trying to hold me back. I sang through the song *Try Anything* by Shakira three times. Once wasn't enough, I needed to sing it through three times, in order to pass through that wall, and feel like I could make it through another day.

Singing has been scientifically proven to lower stress, relieve anxiety, and elevate endorphins which make you feel uplifted and happy. It helps relax muscle tension and decreases the levels of the stress hormone cortisol in the blood stream, and can help take your mind off the day's troubles to boost your mood.[32]

In addition, scientists have identified a tiny organ in the ear called the sacculus, which responds to the frequencies created by singing.[33] The response creates an immediate sense of pleasure, regardless of what the singing sounds like, so you don't have to have an amazing voice to feel the positive effects of singing.

Participants in one study showed significant decreases in both anxiety and depression levels after one month of adding singing to their routine.[34]

So if you find yourself in a rough spot, sing along to an upbeat, positive song. Sing through one song three times, or sing three different positive upbeat songs once. Allow the music to wash through you and feel the healing and invigorating effects immediately lifting mood, and bringing relief. From my own experience, I can say that it really works.

Print out the lyrics so you can sing all the words and choose songs that have lyrics that have meaning to you personally. Here are a few suggested songs to help you create your own list: *Roar* by Katy Perry, *Try Everything* by Shakira, *Waka Waka* by Shakira, *Brave* by Sara Bareilles, *Unwritten* by Natasha Bedingfield, *Fight Song* by Rachel Platten, *Happy* by Pharrel Williams, *Better When I'm Dancin'* by Meghan Trainor, *On Top of the World* by Imagine Dragons, *Believer* by Imagine Dragons, and *You Are Loved* by Stars Go Dim.

5 second rule

One technique that can help you when you are struggling with fear and motivation is to use the 5 second rule which was made popular by Mel Robbins.[35] The 5 second rule is simple, it's like a countdown for a launch. If there's something you know you should do, but need a boost to actually do it, start counting down from 5 like this 5, 4, 3, 2, 1, and then do it immediately.

The idea behind the 5 second rule is simple: if you have an impulse to act on a goal, you must physically move within 5 seconds or fear may set in, and you will talk yourself out of doing it. Remember, you can't control how you feel, but you can always choose how you act.

Boost confidence and mood with a power pose

You can improve your mood in just 90 seconds by doing this one simple trick. Put your chin up, smile (even if you don't feel like it). Pull your shoulders back; stand straight and tall with your hands relaxed at your sides or on your hips. Keep both feet pointing forward, and keep weight even on both legs. Hold this position for 90 seconds.

Research shows that doing these things will not only make you appear more confident and happy; it actually makes you feel more confident and happy.[36]

Furthermore, smiling, even if it's a fake or forced smile, increases the production of mood-enhancing hormones such as dopamine, serotonin, and endorphins which can help us feel better.[37] Charles Darwin was actually the first to hypothesize that there is a connection between body language and our emotions that goes both ways.[38] We smile when we feel good, but we also feel good when we smile. Today that theory is called the facial feedback hypothesis, and it has been verified in study after study after study. The physical expressions of our body language influence our emotional experience.[39, 40]

Even if you don't feel like it, doing the actions will help increase those feelings. If we want to feel happy then we need to smile more. Smiling, even a fake smile, increases the production of mood-enhancing hormones such as dopamine, serotonin and endorphins. If we want to feel confident, then we stand tall and pull our shoulders back. Holding this pose for just 90 seconds slightly increases the level of testosterone, and decreases the level of cortisol. These chemical changes cause an increase in confidence, and a decrease in stress. [41, 42]

Connect with nature

Being in nature, or even viewing scenes of nature, reduces anger, fear, and stress, and increases pleasant feelings. Spending time outside in nature is good for the body and the mind. It helps distract us from problems, and just helps us feel good. [43] Research show that nature not only makes you feel better emotionally, it increases physical well-being by reducing blood pressure, heart rate, muscle tension, and the production of stress hormones. [44,45]

Feel the warmth of the sun and the coolness of the breeze; and feel your body moving as you walk. Hear the birds, or the waves, or the rustle of the grass in the wind. Smell the flowers and the trees, and see the beauty of nature around you. Enjoy a sensory experience in nature, and feel its calming effects.

Take a walk

Virtually any form of exercise can act as a stress reliever. Exercise does wonderful things to help our emotional well-being. [46] It increases the production of endorphins, which are the brain's feel-good neurotransmitters. Walking, jogging, and other forms of exercise that use large muscle groups in a repetitive motion are also forms of moving meditation. These moving meditations provide similar benefits to traditional meditation by calming us down, and distracting us from our problems. It improves mood, builds confidence, helps us relax, and improves quality of sleep.[47, 48, 49] So if you're feeling stressed out, it might be a good idea to pause and go for a walk.[50]

Visualize a shield

If you're struggling with feelings of fear and vulnerability, visualizing a shield can be a way to help you feel safer.[51] Mental creation with intention is a powerful thing. We can invent, create, experience and destroy things with thoughts alone.

Creating a shield basically means imagining, visualizing, intending, and feeling that you are completely surrounded by a force field or shield. Be creative and specific in imagining what it looks like, what color it is, how it feels inside, and any other specific details you can think of. Imagine that negative comments are deflected by the shield. They don't even reach you, and they can't get inside you. You allow them to bounce off into space where they are harmless. Choose to allow positive comments to flow through the shield. The shield is a filter, not a wall.

When I was struggling with feelings of anxiety, I thought that every person and every situation was a potential threat to me, and I was not safe anywhere or with anyone. So I made it a habit to create a shield each morning as a part of my daily routine, just like brushing my teeth. And if I found myself stressed out, overly emotional, or feeling threatened, I would re-apply my shield. I also visualized my shield in preparation for attending any social function where I knew there would be a lot of people. I thought the idea of visualizing a shield sounded a little silly when the idea was first suggested to me, but it really helped as a coping mechanism and with time the fear began to subside.

2-minute distraction

One of unhealthiest and most common forms of negative thinking is called rumination.[52] To ruminate means to chew over. It's when your boss yells at you, or you make an embarrassing mistake, or something scary happens, or you imagine something scary that might happen, and you just can't stop replaying the scene in your head for days, sometimes for weeks on end.

Spending so much time focused on upsetting and negative thoughts, actually puts you at significant risk for developing clinical depression, alcoholism, eating disorders, and even cardiovascular disease.[53]

The problem is, the urge to ruminate can feel really strong, so it's a difficult habit to stop. But there are ways to combat that urge. Studies tell us that even a two-minute distraction is sufficient to break the urge to ruminate in that moment.[54]

If your thoughts are swirling in fear and despair, take action to break free of them and attain a fresh perspective. Become immersed in a great book that moves you, or watch a movie that transports you. Exercise. Go for a walk. In short, do what you know from experience bounces your thinking to a more optimistic place.

If you can succeed in changing your mental channel for at least two minutes, you have a chance of breaking that destructive cycle of rumination. By battling negative thinking, you won't just heal your psychological wounds, you will build emotional resilience, and you will thrive.[55]

Laughter

When looking for an excellent distraction, laughter really is the best medicine. Laughter stops distressing emotions. It helps you shift perspective, allowing you to see situations in a more realistic, less threatening light.

Laughter makes you feel good. It triggers the release of endorphins, the body's natural feel-good chemicals.[56] And the good feeling that you get when you laugh remains with you even after the laughter subsides. Humor helps you keep a positive, optimistic outlook through difficult situations, disappointments, and loss. It adds joy and zest to life, eases anxiety and tension, relieves stress, improves mood, and strengthens resilience.[57]

So what makes you laugh? A good joke? Funny cat videos? Make a list of things that make you laugh and keep them on hand, because nothing works faster, or more dependably, to bring your mind and body back into balance than a good laugh.

Mini-meditation

There are many studies that verify that meditation eases anxiety and mental stress.[58]

Here's a mini meditation exercise that you can do anytime, anywhere, to help calm you down in just a few seconds. With your hands in front of you, line up the tips of the fingers of your left hand to the corresponding tips of the fingers of your right hand. Take 5 slow, deep belly breaths while pressing the fingertips against each other with medium force. Shake out your hands, and relax them to your sides or your lap, and take one last slow, deep breath.

Connect with friends

We live in a digital age where we can be tempted to replace person to person contact with phones and computers, especially if we're feeling vulnerable. But humans are social creatures, we crave feeling supported, valued, and connected. Studies show that being socially connected increases happiness, and leads to better health and a longer life. It helps overcome feelings of loneliness and isolation.[59]

Make a list of the people you can turn to. These are people that you trust to support you, and make an effort to contact them regularly. Reach out to them, and ask for specific kinds of help. Remember, your friends can't read your mind, and it's not fair to expect them to. And if you're working on a goal, such as trying to overcome anxiety and depression, having a friend to report to and keep you accountable can make all the difference in the world. The likelihood of getting new habits to stick, of following through on your assignments, and reaching goals, is remarkably higher when someone else is aware of your goal or assignment, and you set a time to report back to someone on your progress.

Replace rumination with positive affirmations

When we get caught in the trap of rumination, which is repeating negative self-thoughts over and over again, we have to do something to interrupt that cycle or it just keeps going.[60] Rumination is so dangerous because studies show that people believe things that they hear a lot because they are familiar, and disbelieve things that they don't hear because they are unfamiliar.[61] It is interesting because it has no basis in logic.

This is why it is so dangerous when we repeat over and over in our minds things like: "I'm not good enough," "I'm a failure," "I'm not safe," etc. Even though there may be no basis in logical foundation for these statements, we believe them to be true simply because we repeat them to ourselves over and over again.

There is a way to combat these beliefs using the same principle of repetition. By creating positive statements about ourselves and repeating them over and over, it can create a new healthier positive belief system.[62]

So if a thought keeps running through your mind like, "I'm not good enough," replace it with another opposite and positive statement such as, "I am worthy and deserving of being loved, valued and appreciated. I am loved, valued and appreciated. I am good enough." And repeat that over and over again. There's a lot of truth taught in the children's book "The Little Engine That Could" by Watty Piper. Repeating, "I think I can, I think I can," (or whatever positive mantra is applicable) really makes a difference.

It won't be easy however. When you say those things your subconscious may tell you that they're lies. Studies show that once we believe something, we instinctively defend and protect it without even being aware of it.[63] But if we keep at it relentlessly and consistently, that power of repetition can retrain our brains to accept those things as true.[64]

Pet the dog

If you're feeling anxious, stressed, depressed, or lonely, one thing that might help is to spend some time petting a dog or cat.[65] Research shows that playing with, or petting, an animal can reduce stress, and can also help us reduce feelings of isolation, and help us feel more connected.[66] Petting a dog or cat increases oxytocin production in the brain, which lowers stress and increases feelings of happiness. It also decreases production of cortisol, which is a stress hormone, so it works in multiple ways to help you calm down and feel better.[67]

Small act of service

Anxiety, worry, and fear tend to make a person retreat inward. Helping other people can help bring us outside ourselves. It can also help distract us from our own problems, and think about something else. Studies have shown that people who help others have lowered levels of depression and anxiety.[68] In fact, in the research study, service was more effective in making a positive difference in the way participants felt about themselves, than making an effort to pamper themselves, or creating self-esteem goals.[69]

4.

THE MORNING ROUTINE

Morning routine (complete before noon) - about 15 minutes

We're going to begin each morning with a few simple steps to get our day started in the right direction. It will only take about 15 minutes. This should be completed sometime before noon. The morning routine consists of three steps. The first step is to do one thing that boosts your physical health. The next step is a short exercise designed to empower, and the third step is intended to increase feelings of peace and safety. Nourishing, empowering, and calming are excellent ways to recharge each morning. An overview of the morning routine looks like this:

Nourishing the body (choose one)

- Good quality vitamin supplement with B-complex vitamins **or**
- Green smoothie **or**
- Wheatgrass

Empowering (do both)

- Spending 2 minutes focusing on the "I am" poster while listening to music **and**
- Repeating a set of positive affirmations three times while listening to music

Building feelings of peace and safety (choose one)

- Creating a virtual shield **or**
- Loving-kindness meditation

What we're doing and why

The following section explains each step of the morning routine and why we would want to do these things.

Do one simple thing to nourish and support your body

Physical, mental, and emotional health are all interconnected. How you feel physically affects your ability to handle stress. Your diet directly affects how you feel mentally and emotionally as well as physically.[70] Many people have seen tremendous physical, emotional, and mental improvements simply by altering their diets from sugary and nutritionally deficient processed foods to a diet rich with whole grains, organic fruits and vegetables, and quality protein. Also drinking enough water is a simple, effective, but often overlooked tool to improve mental and emotional health. Studies show that even mild dehydration has been shown to negatively affect brain structure and function, negatively impact mood, and trigger fatigue.[71]

Since this is only a thirty-day course, it is unreasonable to expect a complete diet overhaul, especially since drastic changes in diet may cause stress and we're trying to reduce stressors. However, it would be negligent to ignore physical health altogether, so I'm going to ask you to do one simple thing to nourish and support your body each day. You may choose what that one thing will be, and you can change it from time to time if you wish. I'll give a couple suggestions.

Vitamin supplements

Take a good quality multivitamin supplement, especially one with that includes all the B-complex vitamins. Some people have seen a noticeable improvement in the way they feel mentally and emotionally just by including a good quality vitamin supplement to their diet. Their brains just needed the right nutritional tools to work with. The B vitamin family is particularly important for energy and emotional health.[72]

As we're trying to improve our ability to handle stressors, it's important to have good energy levels. Vitamin B helps the body convert the food you eat into glucose, which gives you energy. Most of the energy drinks on the market contain high levels of vitamin B, but they also contain high levels of sugar and caffeine which give a boost of energy followed by a crash.[73] It's better for your body to leave out the sugar and caffeine, and just take the B vitamins. Vitamin B not only affects energy levels, but it affects mental and emotional health as well. A deficiency in vitamin B can cause anxiety, panic, and depression.[74] It affects the nervous system and the red blood cells in our bodies.

There are eight B complex vitamins,[75] but they're not all called "Vitamin B" they have other names including:

- thiamin

- riboflavin

- niacin

- pantothenic acid

- biotin

- vitamin B6 (pyridoxine)

- folate (called folic acid when included in supplements)

- vitamin B12 (cyanocobalamin).

I don't know why they name them that way, and I don't know why there's a vitamin B12 when there are only eight B vitamins, but I do know that vitamin B can make a difference. Deficiencies in vitamin B, particularly vitamins B6 and B12, have been shown in multiple studies to be linked to symptoms of depression and anxiety.[76, 77]

As a word of caution, we need to recognize that not all supplements are the same quality. Low quality supplements aren't very effective. There is a website called multivitaminguide.org that compares the effectiveness of 100 different vitamin brands which may be a useful guide in selecting a good quality supplement.[78]

Green smoothie

If you prefer a more natural approach, you might start the day with a nutritious green smoothie. Research shows that a diet high in vegetables, fruit, legumes, whole grains, and lean protein can help people manage their anxiety.[79, 80] Having a green smoothie for breakfast can be an easy way to get some fruits and veggies in your diet.

Wheatgrass

Another superfood option is wheatgrass. Wheatgrass is a food made from the *Triticum aestivum* plant. It's regarded as a super potent health food with amazing benefits. It's usually consumed as a fresh juice, but it also comes in powdered form or pills.

Wheatgrass is packed with a powerful combination of nutrients that make it extremely useful to your health. It has many therapeutic benefits and is known as complete nourishment. The extensive combination of vitamins and nutrients may make wheatgrass an exceptional choice to enhance your well-being. Wheatgrass has antioxidant, antibacterial, and anti-inflammatory properties.[81]

Wheatgrass contains:

- iron
- calcium
- enzymes
- magnesium
- phytonutrients
- 17 amino acids
- vitamins A, C, E, K, and B complex
- chlorophyll
- proteins

Wheatgrass may improve overall mental function and relieve anxiety. One study found that wheatgrass showed therapeutic benefit in the treatment of Chronic Fatigue Syndrome.[82]

If wheatgrass sounds gross to you, then don't choose that option, but do choose to do one simple thing to nourish and support your body to start off each day.

Empowerment

This next section of the morning routine is designed to generate feelings of empowerment. People who are fearful, anxious, worried, or stressed may not see themselves as powerful. You are more powerful than you may realize, so we're going to work on upgrading those core beliefs by building confidence and self-worth through words, images, music, and the power of repetition.

"I am" poster

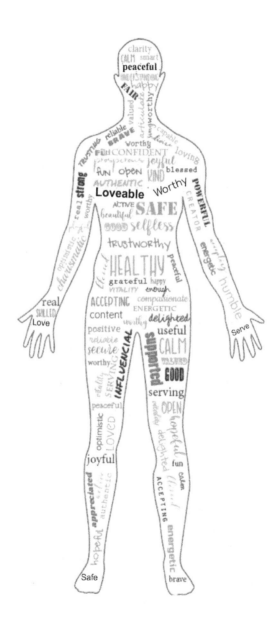

"I am" poster - 2 minutes

Spend two minutes looking at, and pondering about, the "I am" poster included in this book, while listening to inspiring instrumental music. The visual images and words combined in the "I am" poster engages both hemispheres of the brain, and facilitates improvements in reprogramming our patterns of thinking.[83] Adding background music takes it to a whole new level.

The soothing power of music is well established.[84] It affects our emotions and can be an extremely effective stress management tool. Soothing music can slow the pulse and heart rate, lower blood pressure and decrease the levels of stress hormones, and distract us from our worries. Research shows that listening to music can even help a person with clinical depression[85] or bipolar disorder[86] get through their worst, lowest moods.

When people are feeling stressed and overwhelmed, there is a tendency to avoid actively listening to music. Perhaps because it feels like a waste of time when there's so much to do and to worry about. But adding music to our day is a small effort that can produce great rewards, since our productivity[87] actually increases when stress is reduced. Choose background music like the orchestral film music played in the background of your favorite movie. This music is commonly known as "epic music." Just do a quick search on YouTube and you'll have numerous playlist choices available in an instant.

Positive affirmations with music

After your two-minute timer goes off, set down the "I am" poster, and look into a mirror instead. Repeat a set of positive affirmations three times while continuing to listen to your epic background music.

Our beliefs and our thinking are greatly influenced by repetition. Recall our discussion about the mere exposure effect which shows that we are more likely to believe things that we hear over and over again, just because we heard it over and over again, and it doesn't matter if it's true or not. Also remember that once we believe something, whether or not it is true, our subconscious will fight to protect those beliefs by rejecting anything that is unfamiliar or contradicts what we already believe.

These two facts can create a bit of a "Catch 22" situation when trying to upgrade our beliefs from feeling fearful, helpless, and overwhelmed to feeling safe, peaceful, and in control. We need to repeat those things that we'd like to believe over and over again so that we'll believe them; but since the new beliefs contradict the old beliefs, our minds will fight and reject them. You may say the words and find that your subconscious yells, "These are lies!" Don't worry, they're not lies. Those push-back thoughts are just the knee-jerk reaction of the mere exposure effect, as well as that filter in our brain called the reticular activating system (RAS).[88] Just keep going, and those natural warning responses will get over themselves eventually, and join your team after a transition period.

Listening to music while repeating these self-affirmations can help calm those misguided internal warning systems. Music, melody and rhythm can stimulate nerve impulses through the RAS which provides an extra boost to help us get past that filter. This helps speed up the process of transition to accepting a new belief.[89]

Different kinds of music can produce different kinds of emotions, and we can use that to our advantage as well.[90] Some music lets you know that the hero is about to do something, well heroic, and other music lets you know that everything is peaceful and going to turn out okay. Either of these might be just what you need as you repeat your positive affirmations. Perhaps you need a boost of confidence and power, or perhaps you're in the need of a calming reassurance that these new ideas are safe, and that everything is going to be okay.

Repeat your positive affirmations three times with the epic music of your choice playing in the background. Try varying the sound of your voice, speaking confidently and powerfully, or softly and reassuringly to give variety and to wake up the mind, which responds positively to variety.

Please repeat the following positive affirmations three times.

- I am at peace with myself, with others, and with my life circumstances.

- I willingly let go of any unnecessary fear, anxiety, worry, and stress.

- I allow peace, and feelings of safety, to flow into my heart and my mind, and I experience joy and delight each day.

- I am creative, capable, and confident.

- I open my eyes, my mind, and my heart to find solutions to my problems; and I'm delighted that it is easier than I ever thought possible.

Fostering feelings of peace and safety

The next part of the morning routine promotes feelings of peace and safety. There are two options, creating a virtual shield or loving-kindness meditation, so you may choose whichever feels most comfortable for you, or alternate between the two as you see fit.

Imagination is a higher brain function

An article in *Semantic Scholar* by Luca Tateo, explains that imagination is a fundamental psychological higher function that plays a crucial role in scientific thinking as well as in education and promotion of well-being.[91] Tateo says, "Contrary to the traditional understanding in psychology and philosophy, imagination is not in opposition with rational thinking and reality, it is rather a specific form of adaptation and pre-adaptation to environment through a self-regulatory process by production and elaboration of meaning."[92]

We're going to harness some of that power from this higher mental function to imagine and visualize a protective shield. If you're struggling with feelings of fear and vulnerability, visualizing a shield can be a way to help you feel safer. There is a difference between being safe and feeling safe. Some people may think, "I'll feel safe when I can guarantee that I'm actually safe," but that's not necessarily true. Remember that fear can be triggered by real or imagined danger. An interesting study was done by Columbia University in 2012.[93] Their study was about happiness, not necessarily about feeling safe, but the results are applicable to our discussion on feelings of safety as well. They wanted to determine which might be the happiest countries on earth, then deduce what factors might have caused that state of happiness.

Some obvious things to look for would be wealth. People assume they would be happy if only they were rich, but the data didn't match that assumption. Qatar is the richest country in the world, but it ranked number thirty-one in happiness out of the one hundred fifty-six countries they studied. They looked at life expectancy; it seems reasonable that a long life would produce happiness. Japan has the longest life expectancy in the world, but they were forty-fourth on the list of happiness. What about safety? Surely the safest place in the world would be the happiest. Hong Kong had the lowest murder rate of anywhere in the world, but it was number sixty-seven in the happiness ranking.[94] The happiest countries were Denmark, Finland, and Norway, in that order, and none of them could boast the most wealth, the longest life expectancy, or the highest safety rating.

From the study, we see that measurable physical circumstances like wealth, longevity, and physical safety did not determine levels of happiness. The circumstances and the feelings did not necessarily match. Happiness is largely a choice. Feelings of safety and peace can be a choice as well.

Allowing ourselves to feel safe can reduce feelings of anxiety, and help us perform better throughout the day.

Creating your shield

Creating a shield basically means imagining, visualizing, intending and feeling that you are completely surrounded by a force field or shield. Mental creation with intention is a powerful thing.[95] Be creative and specific in imagining what it looks like, what color it is, how it feels inside, what temperature it is, and what it smells like. Notice the quality of the light, and any other specific details you can think of. Imagine that negative comments are deflected by the shield. They don't even reach you, and they can't get inside you. You allow them to bounce off into space where they are harmless. Choose to allow positive comments to flow through the shield. The shield is a filter, not a wall.

From personal experience, I learned that creating a virtual shield is an effective tool to decrease feelings of anxiety. When I was struggling with feelings of anxiety, I thought that every person and every situation was a potential threat to me, and I was not safe anywhere or with anyone. So I made it a habit of creating a shield each morning as a part of my daily routine, just like brushing my teeth, and I found that I was better able to handle the stressors of the day.

Loving-kindness meditation

The second option is to practice loving-kindness meditation. Meditation is a form of somatic quieting and helps to induce the relaxation response. While the virtual shield option is focused primarily on increasing feelings of safety, loving-kindness meditation is more focused on increasing feelings of peace.

We're going to begin with some deep breathing. Some people aren't aware that there are two kinds of breathing, called chest breathing and diaphragmatic breathing. Chest breathing is shallow, and it doesn't fully oxygenate the blood. It may contribute to feelings of anxiety. Diaphragmatic breathing may also be called abdominal breathing, belly breathing, or deep breathing. Diaphragmatic breathing increases the supply of oxygen and nutrients to cells throughout the body. It relieves tension and provides energy to get things done.[96]

To begin, sit upright in a comfortable chair with both feet flat on the floor. Sit up straight and tall, not stiff, but upright. The reason we keep both feet on the floor is that we don't want crossing our legs to cause any blood flow restrictions. We want our blood and our energy to flow freely throughout the body, and we sit up tall for a similar reason. We don't want slouching to restrict our oxygen intake at all. We want to be able to breathe fully and deeply. As we breathe deeply, it enriches our blood with oxygen, which helps feed the cells in our bodies. Place one hand over your chest and the other over your belly. Take a few deep breaths through your nose. Breathing through your nose naturally slows the breathing rate, since the nostrils are smaller openings than your mouth. Notice which hand is moving more. Practice until the hand over your belly is moving, and the hand over your chest is relatively still.

When you have the hang of it, you may rest your hands gently in your lap. Close your eyes to minimize distractions. Take a few deep breaths, and just relax and focus on the gentle sensation of breathing in and out.

Now I want you to pick an image of a person, just a mental image of someone you care about. It can be whoever you like, and just imagine you're looking at that person. While you're focusing on that image, we're going to say a simple mantra, and I want you to imagine that you're saying it to that person.

"May you be free. May you find peace. May you have grace and courage. May you be free. May you find peace. May you have grace and courage. May you be free. May you find peace. May you have grace and courage. May you be

free. May you find peace. May you have grace and courage. May you be free. May you find peace. May you have grace and courage."

Now I'd like you to change the image, and I want you to imagine you're looking in a mirror. So you're looking at yourself as you repeat this mantra. This is a message for you.

"May you be free. May you find peace. May you have grace and courage. May you be free. May you find peace. May you have grace and courage. May you be free. May you find peace. May you have grace and courage. May you be free. May you find peace. May you have grace and courage. May you be free. May you find peace. May you have grace and courage."

Bring your attention back to your breath. Take a few more deep breaths, then gently open your eyes. The morning routine is complete. You're nourished, empowered, and have encouraged feelings of peace and safety. You're ready to face the day.

5.

THE EVENING ROUTINE

Evening routine (complete before midnight) - about 15 minutes

Each day will also include a short evening routine that can be completed in about fifteen minutes. How we begin and end each day is very important. As a general rule, the last things we think about at night run through our minds while we sleep.[97] If we go to bed stressing and worrying, those things may continue to cycle through our brain throughout the night. It is possible to wake up in the morning already feeling tired from mental exhaustion, which makes it really difficult to face a new day. Your evening routine is designed to help you be able to relax and enjoy better quality sleep, which in turn helps you have a better day tomorrow. The evening routine repeats some of the activities from the morning routine including the "I am" poster, and positive affirmations while listening to music. The evening routine finishes off with a progressive relaxation exercise. An overview of the evening routine looks like this:

Empowering

- Spending 2 minutes focusing on the "I am" poster while listening to music

- Repeating a set of positive affirmations three times while listening to music

Somatic quieting through progressive relaxation

What we're doing and why

The following section explains each step of the evening routine and why we would want to do these things. The reasoning behind the "I am" poster and positive affirmations were already explained in the morning routine section. They are a multidimensional approach to increase personal empowerment. Next I'll explain about the somatic quieting through progressive relaxation.

Somatic quieting review

Earlier in the book, I explained that somatic quieting turns on the relaxation response in the body. The relaxation response is essentially the opposite reaction to the stress response. It is a process of turning the "rest and digest" system back on. This releases chemicals and brain signals to make your muscles and organs slow down, and increases blood flow to the brain.

There are many techniques for somatic quieting; we're going to incorporate three of these techniques including diaphragmatic breathing, progressive muscle relaxation, and guided imagery.[99]

The idea behind progressive muscle relaxation is that, often, when we're stressed throughout the day, we hold the tension in our body; but we're often not aware of the stress, so we may have tightness in our shoulders, our neck, our lower back, and so on. We're going to control these muscles by first tensing them up, and then we'll relax them; and by contrasting those two states it helps you to develop more of an awareness of when you're tense and when you're relaxed.

Progressive muscle relaxation exercise

Lie down and get comfortable. First you're going to focus on your breathing. We're going to work on breathing slower and deeper. Take a few deep breaths through your nose. Breathing through your nose naturally slows the rate of breathing, because nostrils are smaller openings than your mouth, and it takes a little longer to inhale and exhale completely. Place one hand on your chest and one hand on your belly. Notice which hand is moving. When we are doing shallow chest breathing, the hand over your chest will move up and down. You also might notice your shoulders moving up and down; but if you're doing deep diaphragmatic breathing then the hand over your belly will move, and the hand over your chest will hardly move at all as you breathe in and out. Practice a few times, feeling that hand over your belly moving up and down. When you feel comfortable that you're doing it well, then you can relax your hands into your lap, or at your sides.

Now, I'd like you to close your eyes to minimize distractions; we're going to give your eyes a rest and use some of your other senses right now.

Let yourself relax. I'm going to ask you to direct your attention to your toes and your feet. Now I'm going to ask you to scrunch up and tighten your toes. Squeeze the muscles in your toes, and feel the tightness. Feel a little bit of that tension in your toes, and hold it, hold it. Hold that tension and that tightness in your toes. And then just relax that tension. Relax your toes. Now imagine a warm wave of relaxation is washing over your toes. This wave of peace and relaxation is lapping at your feet, relaxing your feet and your toes.

Next we're going to move up to your calves. Tighten your calves by flexing your feet, bringing your toes up towards your body. Feel that large muscle getting a bit warmer as it is squeezing. Keep it tight, tight, tight. Feel the tension in your calves; feel that burn as you hold it tight. Then relax. Lower your toes back down, and shake your feet a little. Shake off that tension. Relax your calves and feel the nourishing blood rushing back to the muscles. Relax. Feel that wave of relaxation washing over your feet and your calves.

Next I'm going to ask you to tighten the muscles in your thighs and your backside. Squeeze your legs, and squeeze your bum cheeks together. Tighten all of those muscles and feel the tension. These are the largest muscles in the body. They are powerful. Squeeze and tighten them and hold them tight. Hold it, hold it, and now release all that tension. Allow all of that tightness and tension to leave your body. Notice the feel of the bed beneath you. Right now something else is supporting you, and those muscles in your body can have a rest. And because of that rest, they will be better able to serve you, and support you when you need them again. Right now they just get to relax. Feel that warm wave of relaxation now washing from your toes all the way up to your waist. Feel how these waves nourish your muscles and your body. As each wave recedes, it pulls out more tension and washes it away, and you feel your legs and lower half of your body completely relaxed.

Now we move up to the torso. Tighten your abdominal muscles like you're doing a sit up or a crunch. Tighten and hold these muscles, feeling the tension in your stomach and lower back. Feel the squeeze, feel the tightness, and just hold it. Hold it, hold the tension, and now release and relax the torso. Let it all go. Allow all of that tension to release, and feel a wave of relaxation washing from your toes all the way up to your armpits. It's nourishing. It's relaxing, and as it recedes it pulls out any tension, any tightness, and any toxins that it finds, and it washes them away.

Next we're going to go to your hands and your arms. I want you to make a tight fist. Make a really tight fist. You can feel it in your forearms; you can feel it in your hands. You can feel all the tightness and the tension in your hands and arms. Just feel that squeeze and hold it. Now relax. Open your fist and allow the fingers to wiggle, releasing any tension. Allow your hands to drop back to your sides. Let your fingers relax, let your arms relax. Imagine now that wave of relaxation is washing over your arms, your torso, and your legs. Allow the wave's nourishing and healing power to wash over you, and then notice how as it recedes, it pulls out any remaining tension.

We'll go up to your shoulders, and I want you to raise your shoulders up to your ears. As you tighten these muscles, you feel it in your shoulders; you feel it across your upper back, and you feel it in your neck. Feel the tension, feel the tightness, and hold it. And then release it. Let your shoulders relax. Let your upper back relax. Let your neck relax. Imagine that wave of relaxation again washing from your toes to your neck, feeling it nourishing and relaxing as it washes over you, and pulling out any tension or toxins. This gentle wave is massaging away any tension, leaving the muscles completely relaxed.

Now I want you to tense your face by pressing your lips together and scrunching your nose. Just press it together. Feel the tension, feel the tightness in those facial muscles. Hold it, and then relax. Imagine now that you're in a deep warm bath, completely covered and completely relaxed. As the gentle warmth enfolds you, it nourishes and heals your body and your mind, and washes away any tension.

Direct your attention back to your breath. Take a few nice deep belly breaths, breathing through your nose. Now do a quick scan of your body, starting with your toes and working all the way up to the crown of your head. If there are any remaining spots of tension, imagine another gentle wave of relaxation is coming. This wave is massaging away any tension, and bringing a sense of calm and peace from your head to your toes.

Just continue to relax and breathe deeply, but we're going to help take your mind somewhere - somewhere that brings you peace or brings your joy. I want you to imagine your picture of paradise, a place where you would like to go. Maybe it's on a beach, or in a beautiful meadow, or a cabin in a forest. Wherever brings you peace and happiness.

I want you to look around this place that you're created. This is a place where you are absolutely safe. This is a place that is completely under your control. I want you to notice what's there. I want you to notice if there are other people around or if you're there by yourself. Notice the light. Is it bright, or is it dim? Notice the temperature. Is it warm or is it cool? Notice any smells that are there. Do you smell flowers, pine trees, freshly baked chocolate chip cookies, or something else? Pay attention to any sounds that you might be hearing. Are there birds; is there music? Allow yourself to enjoy a full sensory experience. This is a place that belongs to you. It is your space; you control it, and you can go back to this place any time that you want. It only takes a moment. Allow this place to feed you, to nourish your soul, to take away any stress or pain.

Take a few deep breaths. I want you to take one last look around your personal paradise, and remind yourself that you can come back here any time that you want. You're going to say goodbye for now, but you're going to make a promise to come back sometime soon. Again notice the sights, the sounds, the smells, and make that promise to come back.

Draw your attention back to your breath. Take a few deep, belly breaths, and come back to where you are. Open your eyes, wiggle your fingers and your toes. Your body and your mind are completely relaxed.

Sleep

Let's talk about the importance of sleep. On average, we need to have about seven to eight hours of sleep per night. A wide variety of data suggest that when we don't get enough sleep, it can impair our decision making and affect our emotions. Tests on intelligence, creativity, attention, and memory all show lower performance with sleep deprivation.[100]

There are several stages to our sleep. Stage 1 is a light sleep that begins when you fall asleep. During stage 2 the heart rate slows and the body temperature drops. Stages 3 and 4 are a deep sleep where the body is able to repair itself. The final stage, called REM or rapid eye movement, is the stage where we dream. It takes about ninety minutes for your body to go through one complete sleep cycle and we go through several of these cycles each night.[101]

The following diagram shows the sleep phases during a typical night. The peaks of the waves represent the REM sleep. The sleep phases go in order like this: 1, 2, 3, 4, 3, 2, 1, REM, 1, 2, 3, 4, 3, 2, 1, REM and so on. That would represent two complete sleep cycles. In this diagram notice that during the first sleep cycle, the REM time is very short. It gets a little longer during the second cycle and significantly longer during the third and fourth cycles. This is very important to understand because if you reduce your sleep by a couple hours, you might think that you've still gotten most of a good night's sleep. In terms of total hours that is certainly true. You may have missed out on only about 25 percent of your sleep time, but you may have lost 40 percent of your REM sleep time.[102]

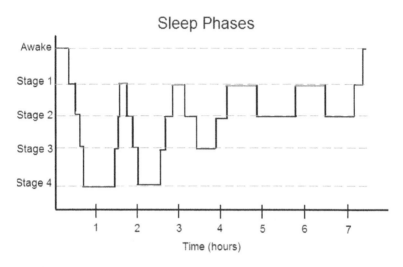

Sleep Phases

REM sleep

Your brain needs REM sleep like it needs nutritious food. Your brain isn't turning off when you go to sleep, rather, it's shifting into a different mode of activity. There is a wealth of evidence that during REM sleep, your brain does essential work that supports regular brain function.[103]

Dreaming is part of the REM phase. According to the National Sleep Foundation, you dream for a total of about two hours during a typical night.[104] That time is not continuous, but divided among the multiple sleep cycles. During the first REM phase, early in the evening, those dreams may be about recent events and they may be very literal, however as the night progresses, the dreams tend to become more abstract.[105] For some reason, this replay and abstraction process is critical to optimal memory, high-level creativity, problem solving ability, and cognitive function, even though we rarely remember those dreams.

In REM deprivation studies, scientists monitored participants while they slept. As soon as participants entered the REM phase, the researchers woke them up, talked for a few minutes and let them go back to sleep. Unfortunately, a person can't just re-enter the sleep cycle at the REM stage; they have to start over again at phase 1. They continued this pattern all night so that although the person had eight hours of sleep, he or she didn't get any REM sleep during that time. Then they observed to see what changes, if any, occurred in the participants' cognitions and behavior. They found that REM deprivation impaired creativity, problem solving abilities, and emotional regulation. They saw an increase in angry outbursts and mood swings. Their brains just didn't function well without experiencing those REM phases.[106, 107]

REM sleep and napping

Napping can be destructive to REM sleep. Most naps are shorter than 90 minutes, which is the time required for a full sleep cycle that includes REM sleep. And even if a nap is 90 minutes, the REM sleep is very short for the first cycle. Taking a nap often reduces the amount of sleep you get the following night, which may significantly reduce the amount of REM time.[108]

What about power napping? Power napping will indeed benefit a person who is sleep deprived. It boosts cognitive functioning in many people, but most of the data about power napping includes participants who were sleep deprived so the data is somewhat skewed. Power napping is indeed better than trying to function when you're sleep deprived, but it's not as good as getting a full night's sleep.[109]

Insomnia

Insomnia is the condition of having trouble falling or staying asleep and affects millions of people. Many turn to prescription sleep medication, and while any sleep is better than no sleep, there is a problem with medicated sleep. Standard sleep medications may disrupt REM sleep.[110]

There are natural supplements, such as melatonin, which may provide a good short term benefit; but our bodies tend to develop a tolerance to these sleep medications over time, and they become less effective.[112] Research shows that the best way to combat insomnia is to work in harmony with the body's natural systems.[113]

Our sleep is influenced by multiple sources, including our circadian rhythms, but that's not all. Research, by Jesus A. Tapia and colleagues in 2013, supported the hypothesis that the reticular activating system (RAS) mediates the transition between sleep and wakefulness.[114] We've talked about the RAS before in another context. We know that it is the gateway into the brain, and it selectively filters incoming sensory information and organizes it into conscious thought. It is the brain's attention center. It influences what we pay attention to. We also know that the RAS functions on subconscious programs, but we can effectively change its programming by altering our thoughts and behaviors if the current programming is not serving us well.[115, 116] Therefore, if we're struggling with falling asleep and staying asleep, there are things we can do to retrain the RAS to promote better sleep.

Habits that may negatively affect sleep

Dr. Peter Vishton, a professor at William and Mary College, suggests that the best way to combat insomnia is to strengthen your unconscious association between your bedroom and sleep.[117] Researchers observe that a majority of people who struggle with insomnia are also using their bedrooms as a place for watching movies, working on the computer, making phone calls, and/or eating.[118] The unconscious systems that regulate your sleep associate these non-sleep activities with your bed, and conclude that going to bed doesn't necessarily mean sleep; it might mean working, playing, or thinking.

Screen time is particularly disrupting to the systems that tell your body to sleep. The internal clock inside our brain is designed to wake up when it is light. It has receptors that are particularly sensitive to blue light. When this blue light strikes the receptors, it disrupts the internal clock function, and it reduces your brain's release of melatonin, which is the chemical in our body that promotes sleep.[119]

Furthermore, blue light doesn't always look blue. White light contains a mix of many wavelengths of light, including blue, and it has the same effect on the receptors in the brain.[120] Light signals the brain that it's time to get up, not that it's time to go to sleep.

Tips to promote a good night's sleep

Good sleep habits (sometimes referred to as "sleep hygiene") can help you get a good night's sleep.[121] Here are a few suggestions that can improve your sleep health.[122]

- Turn your bedroom into a sleep haven. Make sure that it is orderly and comfortable. Remove televisions and computers. Strengthen your unconscious association between your bedroom and sleep. It's best if the activities in the bedroom are limited to sleeping and sex. Make your room peaceful and conducive to sleeping by keeping it quiet, cool, and dark. Earplugs are helpful if you live in a noisy area. Outside light can keep you awake, so try room-darkening shades. Get a good quality mattress and pillow. You spend nearly one third of your life in bed, so this is a place that is worthy of a good investment.

- Exercise during the day. There is solid evidence that regular exercise can improve the quality and duration of sleep. But don't do it right before bed, unless perhaps your choice of exercise is yoga.

- Dim or turn off the lights at least 30 minutes before going to bed.

- Turn off computer screens, televisions, phone screens, etc. at least 30 minutes before going to bed.

- Don't take naps during the day. But if you find that you just need a nap to make it through the day, take a quick 30-minute power nap, so that it will be less likely to interfere with sleeping at night.

- Follow a consistent schedule. Going to sleep and waking up at the same time every day is crucial for setting your body's internal clock (circadian rhythm). Staying consistent also means that the quality of your sleep will be better.

- Avoid alcohol, caffeine, and nicotine for at least four hours before bedtime so you'll have time for the effects to wear off. Although alcohol can help you feel sleepy, it decreases the quality of sleep.

- Follow a consistent evening routine. Having a repeated relaxing ritual that you do every night will signal your body that it's time to settle down. For the next 30 days, I have an evening routine mapped out for you. After that, you may continue that same routine or choose any number of relaxing activities to create your own routine. Reading, listening to calming music, or taking a warm bath are excellent choices. Remember that watching TV, looking at laptops, tablets, or smartphone screens trigger your brain to stay awake, so it's best to stop doing these activities at least 30 minutes before going to bed.

Ways to get back to sleep if you wake up during the night

Sometimes we find ourselves wide-awake during the night and struggle to drift back to sleep. Here are some ideas to help you fall back to sleep.[123]

- Avoid your phone. If you find yourself wide-awake and struggling to drift back to sleep, don't reach for your phone to scroll through Facebook, check email, or play video games. Remember that light from screens sends a signal to your body that it's time to be awake regardless of what time it is. Also these activities can easily suck you in for longer than you intended.

- Cover the clock. Constantly checking to see what time it is, how long you've been awake, or how many minutes and hours are left until morning can cause stress and anxiety to build, making it difficult to fall back asleep. Before you know it, you're stuck in a frustrating cycle where your inability to sleep causes stress and your stress keeps you from sleeping. Turn your clock toward the wall or toss a shirt over it to keep yourself from sneaking a peek.

- Get out of bed if you find yourself tossing and turning for long periods of time. Go to a different room and do a quiet, soothing activity like reading a book or sipping a cup of herbal tea. Keep the lights dim to remind your body that it's still night time, and when your eyelids start to droop try going back to bed. Although getting out of bed may seem counterintuitive when you're desperately trying to fall asleep, changing to a different location can help prevent the mind from creating a negative association between the stress of not sleeping and the space you are lying in.

Practice relaxing. Progressive muscle relaxation is one way to get your mind and body to relax. Another is to practice deep breathing. You could even try counting backwards from 100 to interrupt racing thoughts. The goal is to focus on the present moment, and let go of ruminating thoughts or any tension that might be keeping you awake.

6.

DAILY ACTION STEPS

In addition to the morning routine, each day we will be taking simple action steps that can be completed any time during the day. These action steps should take thirty minutes or less. These will change each day, but I'll explain what to do and why to do it every step of the way.

Day 1 – Journaling to reduce fear, anxiety, worry, and stress

Today's action step is a journaling exercise. Journaling is a great tool for coping with fear, anxiety, worry, and stress.[124] There are many different types and purposes of journaling. Today we're just going to take those worries and fears, and get it out on paper.

Why we're doing this exercise

Imagine an over-inflated balloon; you can see the strain on the surface and know that it will explode at the slightest provocation. However, if some of the pressure is released from the balloon, it becomes much more pliable and resilient.

Likewise, if we're over-inflated with fear, anxiety, worry, and stress, we can feel overwhelmed with the strain and pressure. However, if some of the emotional pressure is released, we become more pliable and resilient. We can better handle whatever situation we're in.

There is a saying that "a burden shared is a burden halved," and today we're going to relieve burdens by sharing them with a pen and paper. Multiple studies suggest that journaling is good for your mental health because it makes you more aware, improves perspective, and helps make problems feel more manageable.[125]

Journaling exercise instructions - Spend 20-30 minutes writing on one or more of the following prompts:

- I feel fearful because…

- I feel anxious because…

- I feel worried because…

- I feel stressed because...

List everything you can think of. Just put the pen to paper and write whatever comes to your mind.

Journaling and emotions

This may be an emotional experience. When we remember an event, our brain actually includes all the experiences that go with it, including how we felt at the time. Emotional states are part of our system of memory encoding and processing.[126]

Dr. Peter Vishton, a professor of Psychology at William and Mary, teaches that human memory is often described in terms of two separate brain systems: short term memory and long term memory.[127] When something happens to you, the event is first stored in short term memory, and if you want to remember it for a long time, it is then transferred from short term into long term.[128] In some ways, it's like a computer. Our short term memory is like a computer's random access memory (RAM) and the long term memory is like the computer's hard drive. Your short term memory has limited capacity, but it's easily accessed. The long term memory may take longer to respond, but it can store a considerable quantity of data.[129]

When you create a long-term memory, you encode the specific information as well as extra, related details. For example, you might recall external details such as the place and time of day. You also record your internal state of being, like your emotions including anger, fears, worries, and anxieties.[130] Studies have shown that these attached emotions can even be passed to the next generation through DNA.[131]

When you remember something, the process reverses; the memory goes from long term, to short term so we can access it. It's sort of like checking it out of a memory library. When we recall an event, we also recall the emotions attached to those experiences which have been recorded in your body.[132]

Now comes the exciting part, research done by Dr. Merel Kindt and colleagues at the University of Amsterdam shows that when a memory is "checked out" of our long term memory it is placed in a state of flux, a state in which it can be changed.[133] The event and the emotion are checked out as a group, but they can be separated, and when we check the memory back into the memory library it no longer has that negative emotion attached.[134] This process may be referred to as memory reconsolidation intervention.[135]

This means that there is a way to keep our memories and remove whatever scary, awful emotions we may have experienced at the time. Dr. Kindt uses this groundbreaking research to treat phobias and PTSD.[136] It might be a painful process to recall the event, which will initially also recall its attached powerful emotions; but with effort, the hurtful feelings can be released, and we don't have to store them in our bodies anymore.

Somatic quieting

Because this journaling exercise may bring up negative emotions, which in turn may activate the body's stress response, we're going to do some somatic quieting afterwards to calm the body and the mind. You may choose from a couple of different options. You may try a mini-meditation, repeat either the virtual shield or loving-kindness meditation from the morning routine, or even something else that you know from experience helps you turn on that relaxation response.

How to do a mini-meditation

There are many studies that verify that meditation eases anxiety and mental stress.[137] Here's a mini meditation exercise that you can do anytime, anywhere, to help calm you down in just a few seconds. With your hands in front of you, line up the tips of the fingers of your left hand to the corresponding tips of the fingers of your right hand. Take five or more slow, deep belly breaths while pressing the fingertips against each other with medium force. Feel the pressure of the fingertips pressing together. Then shake out your hands, and relax them to your sides or your lap, and take a few more slow, deep breaths.

Day 2 - Connect with nature and/or exercise

The action step for today is to dedicate 30 minutes to calm the body and mind either by exercising, or by connecting with nature, and preferably by combining the two. My first choice would be to take a walk through some beautiful natural scenery, whether that be in a park, along a beach, a river trail, a mountain path, or just around the neighborhood.

Exercise relieves stress

Virtually any form of exercise can act as a stress reliever,[138] but activities such as walking or jogging that involve repetitive movements of large muscle groups can be particularly stress relieving, since they offer many of the same benefits as meditation. The benefits are strongest when you exercise regularly. People who exercise regularly are less likely to experience anxiety than those who don't exercise.[139]

There are a few reasons behind this. Regular exercise lowers the level of stress hormones. It also helps release endorphins, which are chemicals that improve your mood and act as natural painkillers.[140] Exercise can also improve your sleep quality, which can be negatively affected by stress and anxiety.[141] Regular exercise improves feelings of confidence and mood, which in turn promotes mental wellbeing.[142]

Try to find an exercise routine or activity you enjoy, such as walking, dancing, rock climbing, or yoga to relieve stress, worry, and anxiety.[143]

Being in nature reduces stress

Studies show that just 20 minutes of contact with nature will significantly lower your stress hormone levels.[144] Spending time outside in nature is good for the body and the mind. It helps relieve feelings of worry, anxiety, and stress. Natural beauty distracts us from problems and just helps us feel good. Studies show that being in nature, or even viewing scenes of nature, reduces anger, fear, and stress, and increases pleasant feelings. Exposure to nature not only makes you feel better emotionally, it contributes to your physical well-being, reducing blood pressure, heart rate, muscle tension, and the production of stress hormones.[145, 146]

If the weather permits, take off your shoes and feel the grass or sand under your feet to enhance your sensory experience. The more senses you can engage the better. Feel the warmth of the sun, feel the cool of the breeze, and feel your body moving as you walk. Hear the birds, or the waves, or the rustle of the grass in the wind. Smell the flowers and the trees, and see the beauty of nature around you. Allow yourself to be in the moment. This is also called being present, or being mindful. Mindfulness is achieved by focusing awareness on the present moment. Mindfulness is a proven method of reducing fear, anxiety, worry, and stress.[147] Often our minds are worrying about the future, or the past, or both. Mindfulness is temporarily letting go of the past and the future, and simply enjoying the present.

Many of us find it difficult to sit still and simply choose to clear our minds of past, present, and future stressors. But if we're walking in nature and noticing the beauty around us, it's easier to let go just for a little while and be present, which then empowers us to be better able to handle our challenges when we pick them up again. Research verifies that connecting with nature is calming.[148] It helps us feel good. The more we can connect with it the better.

Adapt as necessary

This activity will obviously vary depending on season, location, or current weather conditions. If you can't go outside and take a walk, then just adapt and do the best you can. Be creative. What can you do to create an interaction with nature? If you need to be indoors, you can do a mall-walk, or use a treadmill, and walk for 30 minutes while listening to headphones with the sounds of birds, waves, or other nature sounds. Many grocery stores have a floral department. Walk around the store, and then literally stop and smell the roses. Just do the best you can.

Another option is to listen to a recording of nature while grooming a desktop Zen garden or executive sandbox. These tiny boxes of sand with a miniature rake are thought to help increase mindfulness and meditation. It's believed that raking the sand of these desk Zen gardens and creating swirling patterns help calm your mind. Tending these mini landscapes can be a great escape, if even for just a few minutes.[149]

Pet therapy

Another possible connection with nature is to spend time with an animal. Research shows that playing with or petting an animal can reduce stress.[150] It increases levels of the stress-reducing hormone oxytocin, and decreases production of the stress hormone cortisol, and helps overcome feelings of isolation and loneliness.[151]

If this is your best option, then just enjoy 30 minutes petting, playing with, and interacting with your pet.

Whichever option you choose is fine. We will be doing this more than once, so you may choose to mix it up and try different things on different days.

Day 3 – Journaling to reduce fear, anxiety, worry, and stress

Today's action step is a journaling exercise. Journaling is a great tool for coping with fear, anxiety, worry, and stress. This is a repeat of the activity done on day 1. If you need a refresher of what to do and why, please review the instruction for day 1.

Day 4 - CBT triangle

CBT is an abbreviation for "cognitive behavioral therapy." Cognitive behavioral therapy is a form of psychological treatment that teaches that our thoughts, emotions, and behaviors are all interconnected with each other and influence one another. Therefore, we can change, or at least influence, one by changing another. CBT has been demonstrated to be effective for a range of problems including depression, anxiety disorders, alcohol and drug use problems, marital problems, eating disorders, and severe mental illness. Numerous research studies suggest that CBT leads to significant improvement in functioning and quality of life.[152, 153]

Today's action step is to increase personal awareness by using a CBT triangle. A CBT triangle is simply a diagram that shows how our thoughts, emotions, and behavior are all interconnected with each other and influence one another. When you record your thoughts, include the following categories: thoughts about self, thoughts about others, and thoughts about the world in general.

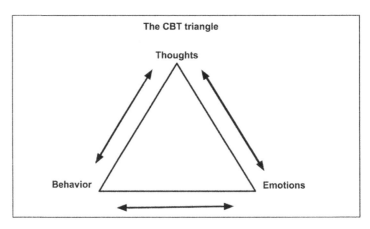

I'll give an example of how this chart is filled out by using one of the stories that I shared in the introduction section. Recall the story of the dreaded phone calls where I was assigned to make phone calls to people I didn't know, and set up appointments to meet with them. In this experience some of my emotions included: fear, dread, worry, anxiety, and stress.

Some of my thoughts about myself were, "I don't want to do this," "I don't like talking to strangers," and "I don't know what to say." Some of my thoughts about other people were, "They don't want to talk to me," "They're going to reject me," and "They might not like me." Some of my thoughts about the world in general were, "The world is scary and unsafe." Some of my behaviors included: avoidance, procrastination, and finally making the calls. I will use this information to fill in the CBT triangle.

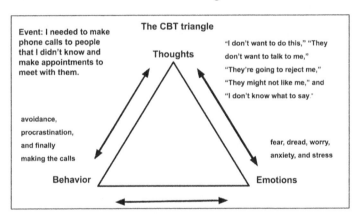

From the arrows on the triangle you'll notice that the thoughts, emotions, and behaviors are all interconnected, and they influence each other. I thought that the people wouldn't like me, didn't want to talk to me, and might reject me, which filled me with fear, dread, worry, anxiety, and stress; so I avoided and procrastinated doing the task. The avoidance and procrastination filled me with fear and dread, because the task still needed to be done, but I hadn't done it yet; and led to thoughts like, "I don't want to do this," and so on. My emotions of fear, dread, anxiety, etc. led to thoughts like, "I don't want to do this," "They're going to reject me," and so on. My fearful emotions also led me to task avoidance and procrastination. So you can see that the thoughts influence the emotions and behavior, the emotions influence the thoughts and behavior, and the behavior influences the thoughts and emotions. They are all interconnected and influence each other.

Today's action step is to choose a recent event and use that event to fill in a CBT triangle. What were your thoughts? What were your emotions? What were your behaviors? This exercise increases awareness of how your emotions, thoughts, and behaviors are interconnected.

Day 5 - Cognitive distortions chart

For today's action step you're going to analyze some of your thoughts and see if there are any cognitive distortions. When something happens to us, we usually have thoughts that automatically come to mind. These automatic thoughts are often done out of habit and we don't even realize that we're doing it. Unfortunately, these automatic thoughts usually include assumptions or patterns often called "cognitive distortions," because they don't accurately reflect what's going on.[154, 155]

The following is a list of possible cognitive distortions that we might use, as well as questions we might ask ourselves, in order to give a more balanced and accurate perspective:

- <u>Personalization</u> is the tendency to take everything very personally. This can either come in the form of assuming that something was intended as a personal attack, or it might manifest in a belief that everything that happened is all our fault. We're personally to blame for everything.

  o Balancing question - Is there another way of looking at this? Who or what else may have played a part in this?

- <u>Selective attention/mental filtering</u> is the tendency to focus on negative events, while filtering out or ignoring the positive events, or things that went well.

  o Balancing question - What are the positives in this situation? Did anything go right?

- <u>Fortune telling</u> is a form of jumping to conclusions, where we assume we know what will happen in the future. Usually fortune telling includes pessimistic thinking or what could go wrong.

- o Balancing question - What evidence do I have to support this conclusion? Is there another possible outcome?

- Mind reading is another form of jumping to conclusions, where we assume that we know what someone else is thinking. These conclusions are rarely, if ever, based on facts or concrete evidence; but rather based on personal feelings and opinions. As a result, they can often lead us astray.

    - o Balancing question - What evidence do I have to support this conclusion? Is there any evidence that supports a different conclusion? Can I clarify with this person what they're actually thinking?

- Catastrophizing is the tendency to blow circumstances out of proportion, and make things out to be a lot worse than they should be; basically we're making mountains out of molehills. It's helpful to gain perspective by asking yourself a few questions: How bad is this? Can I survive this? Is it permanent? Is it temporary?

    - o Balancing question - Is it possible that things aren't as bad as I make them out to be?

- Overgeneralization is when we tend to make broad generalizations that are based on a single event, and minimal evidence. A clue that we might be using overgeneralization, is when we use phrases that include the words *never* or *always*. For example, "You always…" or "He never…" In these instances, we are using a past event to predict all future events.

- o Balancing question - Can I think of any instances where that was not the case? Is any evidence suggesting that things could now be different?

- <u>Labeling</u> is the tendency to make global statements about ourselves or others, based on behavior in a specific situation. For example, "I'm a failure!" or, "You are an insensitive jerk." It changes a specific behavior or incident, and turns it into an all-encompassing definition. I/you/he/she/they = _____.

  - o Balancing questions - Is there evidence that this is true in all situations? Can I think of any evidence that is contrary to this conclusion?

- <u>Shoulding and musting</u> is the tendency to make unrealistic and unreasonable demands on yourself and others. "I should have done this," or, "She should have done that." This is unhelpful because it sets people up for failure, and also doesn't take into account other alternatives.

  - o Balancing question - Is there another way to do things that I haven't yet considered? Might there be more than one way to do things?

- <u>Emotional reasoning</u> is a cognitive distortion where we tend to interpret our experience of reality, based upon how we are feeling in the moment. Our emotional state skews our interpretation of the actual event.

  - o Balancing question - Is there any evidence that how I'm seeing this isn't accurate? Is it possible that my emotions affected my interpretation of what really happened?

- <u>Magnification and minimization</u> is a cognitive distortion where we tend to magnify the positive attributes of another person, while minimizing our own positive attributes. We often compare someone else's highlight reel with our blooper reel. This devalues ourselves while putting someone else on a pedestal.

  o Balancing question - What talents and abilities do I have? Find evidence that you, too, are deserving and capable.

- <u>Black and white/All-or-nothing</u> thinking refers to thinking in extremes. You are either a success or a failure. Your performance was totally good or totally bad. If you are not perfect, then you are a failure. This binary way of thinking leads to unreasonable expectations, and low self-esteem, and/or harsh criticism of others.

  o Balancing question - What are the positives in this situation? Did anything go right? Is it possible that rather than being entirely black or white, it was actually a shade of gray?

I don't know about you, but I've personally been guilty of making every single one of those cognitive distortions many times over. Let's quickly review the dreaded phone call scenario. Some of my thoughts were, "I don't want to do this," "They don't want to talk to me," "They're going to reject me," "They might not like me," and "I don't know what to say."

How many examples of cognitive distortions can I find? Well, I was definitely using personalization, I thought if someone said 'no,' it meant a personal attack on me and my value, and that the person didn't like me. I used selective attention by only seeing the negative in the situation, while ignoring the times when people were nice and said yes, or were even excited to have someone care about them enough to come and visit them. I used fortune telling, assuming that the future was going to be awful and assuming I would be rejected.

I used catastrophizing, by making mountains out of molehills. It was just a phone call; it was not like my life was being threatened. I used overgeneralization, with ideas like, "I *always* get rejected." I used labeling, in the thoughts and ideas that I was an unlikeable failure. I used lots of shoulding and musting, in that I knew I *should* have been doing something and that it *should* have been easy. I used emotional reasoning, since my interpretation of events was highly colored by my negative emotions. I used all-or-none thinking, and allowed one rejection to mean that I was a failure, rather than looking at a balanced picture including positive and negative.

So as you do this exercise, please don't think there's any criticism or judgment involved. This is about increasing awareness that our thoughts may not be an accurate reflection of what is really happening. Much of our fear, anxiety, worry, and stress can be alleviated simply by getting a more balanced perspective.

Today's action step is to take the thoughts recorded on yesterday's CBT triangle, and see if you can find any cognitive distortions associated with any of those thoughts.

Day 6 – Perfectionistic tendencies chart

The action step for today is designed to increase awareness by filling out a chart that lists evidence for, and evidence against, perfectionistic tendencies. One of the cognitive distortions that we learned about yesterday is so prevalent and complicated that it deserves further discussion. The idea of black and white thinking or all-or-none thinking also goes by another name. It is called perfectionism.[156]

Perfectionism is not the same as striving for excellence (or striving for perfection). Striving for excellence has high expectations and includes a pattern of trying, making mistakes, and trying again. Each day we do our best, and as we continue to do our best, our "best" gradually becomes better. Striving for excellence is not stagnant; it involves movement and progression in a positive direction. It is based on a foundation of confidence, courage, hope, hard work, and patience.

Perfectionism, on the other hand, is a counterfeit to striving for excellence; and like most counterfeits, it looks enough like the real thing to confuse some people. Perfectionism also has high expectations, but there are only two options: perfection (meaning being without flaw) or failure. Every day, and in every circumstance, we must be without flaw. If we make a mistake in any way, then we have failed. Perfectionism is not interested in progression; it's more about arriving and staying in one place. It's about trying to reach a perfect spot and holding that position. Perfectionism relies on self, and is based on a foundation of pride, self-doubt, and fear. There is fear of failure, fear of what other people will think, and fear of not being good enough.[157]

Drawbacks to Perfectionism

Perfectionism can lead to several limiting actions. First of all, perfectionism can block us from acting and moving forward. We want to be perfect, which means we can't make a mistake, so we want to know everything and understand everything *before* we act. But it's pretty hard to really know everything and understand everything, so we shut down, and don't start at all. "I don't think I can do it perfectly, so why try?" Or, "I know I'm just going to fail, so why try? It's much safer to stay here." Remember perfectionism believes perfection is a place, like a magic circle, and we don't want to risk doing anything where we might step outside of the circle. Sometimes perfectionism shows itself in giving up. We try and then fail, so we quit. If we can't do it right the first time, then we certainly don't want to try it again.

Perfectionism can also lead to being critical and judgmental. This can come from two different sources. On the one hand, if I'm feeling like I'm not as good as someone else, I may want to justify myself by searching for ways to tear them down, so they're not above me. If I'm not perfect, then you can't be perfect either. This is like the crab in a pot analogy. You may have heard that if you put one live crab in a pot, the crab can climb out of the pot and get away; but if you put two crabs in a pot then neither of them can get away because if one starts to climb, then the other will pull him back. So if we're being like a crab in a pot, and we're feeling jealous of someone else, then the natural response is to be critical and judgmental about that person; so that, at least in our minds, they're still on the same level that we are.

There's another direction that perfectionism can lead to being critical and judgmental, and that is when we think that we are *better* than somebody else. Because of our superior position, we get to point out everybody else's flaws so that they can fix them. Just FYI, nobody likes or appreciates that, but nevertheless, some people feel very justified in their criticism and judgment. They sincerely believe they're doing people a favor by criticizing and judging other people's flaws. This goes back to a basic premise of perfectionism, which is relying on yourself. People who are following the method of perfectionism believe, "It's my job to be perfect, and it is my job to perfect those around me."

Social comparison theory

Whether a person is critical and judgmental of someone they think is better than them, or someone they think is worse than them, a key factor is the process of comparing. Perfectionism naturally leads to social comparison. In 1954, psychologist Leon Festinger proposed the social comparison theory which studies this tendency to compare ourselves with others and seeks to find some answers as to why we do it.[158, 159] He concluded that humans have an innate drive to evaluate our opinions and our abilities, and also a drive to improve our abilities. If we don't have an objective means to evaluate those things, then we compare them with other people's abilities and opinions.

Perfection is an objective way to evaluate our abilities; something is either perfect, or it's not. It either has flaws or it doesn't. Perfectionists try to measure themselves against that measuring stick, but the truth is that no one can actually do it. We all make mistakes. But perfectionists are desperate to evaluate their abilities, so they turn to the next best alternative, which is to compare them with other people's abilities. In general, there are two kinds of social comparison: upward social comparison and downward social comparison. Upward social comparison is when we compare ourselves with those who we believe are better than us, and downward social comparison is when we compare ourselves with those who we believe are worse off than ourselves.[160]

Is there any benefit to comparing with others?

This idea of comparing ourselves to other people, whether we believe they are above us or below us, comes very naturally, but does it help us or hurt us? My answer is, it depends. It depends on *why* we're comparing ourselves in the first place. Are we comparing to objectively evaluate our abilities, or are we comparing to determine our value and our worth?

Let me explain a little about how those are different. If we're comparing ourselves with other people for self-evaluation and growth, it's about asking questions like, "How am I doing?" and, "Is there something I can learn, or do better, from watching what other people are doing?" If this is the purpose for the comparison, then yes, comparing can be a good thing. It's about looking for role models, and it can help make us better. This sounds a lot like striving for excellence; it involves movement and progression in a positive direction, but typically that is not what a perfectionist is looking for.

Perfectionists are more interested in reaching a perfect spot and holding that position. That sounds a lot more like the other reason for social comparison, and that is comparing ourselves to others in order to determine our self-worth, and particularly to boost our self-esteem. In other words, we're looking for evidence to prove we're good enough.[161]

***Upward Social Comparison* motivation and outcome**

When comparing upward, a person who is striving for excellence might see someone else's success and think, "Oh, that's cool, how can I do that?" They might follow their example, or even ask that person to mentor them so they can learn more. They use upward comparisons to improve their current level of ability.[162]

On the other hand, a person who uses social comparison to evaluate or enhance their own self-worth feels dissatisfaction, anger, jealousy, envy, personal failure, justification, blame, and/or resentment when they see someone that they think is better than them.[163]

Downward social comparison motivation and outcome

When comparing downward, a person who is striving for excellence might see someone they feel is worse off than they are, and respond with feelings of accomplishment and gratitude as they realize how far they've progressed. They typically show compassion for people beneath them, and seek ways to help and encourage them.[164]

However, when a person is using social comparison to determine their value and boost their self-esteem, it has a very different outcome. They tend to look down on other people in order to make themselves feel better about their abilities and their self-worth. They might think, "Well I may not be great at something, but at least I'm better than someone else." They rejoice when other people fail, because prideful comparison says that if you fail, then I succeed.

> "You may be using social comparison to determine your self worth or to boost your self esteem without realizing that you're doing it."

How can you tell?

You may be using social comparison to determine your self-worth or to boost your self-esteem without realizing that you're doing it. How can you determine which purpose and motivation you have for comparison? It's really quite simple. How do you feel when you compare yourself to others? If your comparisons lead you to feel grateful, content, compassionate, inspired, or motivated to become better, then you are using social comparison to strive for excellence.[165]

However, if your comparisons lead you to feel envy, coveting, jealousy, anger, resentment, blame, justification, judgmentalness, bias, dissatisfaction, hatred, guilt, anxiety, or feelings of failure, then you are using prideful comparison to determine your self-worth and to build your self-esteem, *even* if you don't realize that that is what you're doing.

Prideful comparison is not good for anyone, but research shows that it is especially damaging to those who are currently struggling with low self-esteem or depression.[166] So here's a question for you, how do you *feel* after you've spent time on Facebook, Instagram, and/or other social media? If spending time on social media leads you to compare yourself with others, and makes you feel discouraged, stressed, or dissatisfied with your life, then I suggest that you severely limit your time on those platforms. It is a source of stress for you.

Increasing awareness of perfectionistic tendencies

Later in the book, we'll look at more reliable sources for determining self-worth, and building confidence and self-esteem; but for today our assignment is simply becoming aware of perfectionistic tendencies. The action step is to fill out a chart that lists evidence for, and evidence against, perfectionistic tendencies.

Day 7 - Connect with nature and/or exercise

Today's action step is to spend 30 minutes connecting with nature and/or exercising. If you need a reminder of what to do, or why to do it, please review the information for day 2.

Day 8 - Discovering perceived rewards

Today's action step is a journaling exercise to dig a little deeper for answers. We're actively looking for ways to reduce fear, anxiety, worry, and stress, but sometimes we're reluctant to let those emotions go. Today's assignment is designed to help us become aware of how these emotions may be serving us, by taking a deeper look at our core beliefs.

How do these emotions serve us?

It may seem strange that we would want to hold onto feelings of fear, anxiety, worry, and stress; but remember from our earlier discussion that emotions by themselves are neither good nor bad, instead they are either helpful or hurtful, depending on intensity, duration, and circumstances.[167] These emotions are intended to help us be safe and successful by heightening awareness, increasing arousal, and boosting our performance level. Remember the Yerkes-Dodson law which shows how stress and arousal actually improve our performance up to a certain point. However, if they get out of hand, they may interfere with our performance, and harm our health, performance, relationships, and happiness.

On a subconscious level, we understand that these emotions serve us; they are giving us some kind of real or perceived benefit. Often it has to do with feelings of safety. Remember that on a primal level, fear-based emotions are intended to keep us safe by heightening awareness and improving performance. Sometimes we misinterpret this, and conclude that the emotions of worry, fear, or anxiety are actually what is keeping us safe. If we worry hard enough, then the bad thing won't actually happen.

> Sometimes we misinterpret this and conclude
> that the emotions of worry, fear or anxiety
> are actually what is keeping us safe.

Mothers are often guilty of this misinterpretation. On some level, they believe that if they worry enough about their children, then it will keep them safe. Even though chronic worry can cause a host of mental, emotional, and physical problems, a mother who believes that worrying will keep her children safe will not allow herself to give up worrying. She does it because she is willing to sacrifice her own health and well-being to protect her children.

Some people believe that fear, anxiety, worry, and stress are expressions of love. Worry is concern coupled with fear. It is possible to love, care, and be concerned about a person without adding fear into the mix. Fear is an integral part of worry, but not everyone understands that. They believe that if I care about someone, then I worry about them. Therefore, the more I worry, the greater my expression of love. Again, even though chronic worrying can ruin a person's life, they continue to do it because they are willing to sacrifice themselves for the people they love.

Although these deep seated beliefs have good and noble intentions, it doesn't actually work that way. Chronic worry, fear and/or anxiety do not protect us or the people we care about. Instead it harms us mentally, emotionally, and physically, and can damage relationships with the people we care about.

Journaling exercise - Discovering perceived rewards

Chances are, you don't actually know what real or perceived rewards you are receiving from fear, anxiety, worry, and/or stress. So here are a few additional questions to help you discover the answers to these questions.

Please spend 20-30 minutes writing on one of more of the following prompts:

- What would be the results if I stopped worrying, feeling anxious, stressed, and/or fearful? What would happen to me? What would happen to the people that I care about?

- Do I feel that worrying about someone demonstrates my love and concern for that person?

- Do I feel guilty if I'm not constantly worrying, stressed or anxious?

Day 9 - Taking a deeper look at core beliefs

We've discussed the idea that the emotions of fear, anxiety, worry, and stress, all give a reward, whether it is real or perceived. These emotions serve us in some way. As we identify what those rewards are, then we may choose whether or not we're willing to let them go in order to receive a better reward. In order to illustrate this point further, I'd like to share a story.

Adelaide wins a prize

My husband was playing with some of our grandchildren. He had a handful of treats, and the game was that the kids had to say the secret password, "I love you Grandpa," in order to get a treat.

Four-year-old Andreas smiled with the delight of a shared secret as he called out, "I love you Grandpa," and was rewarded with a treat. Even two-year-old John quickly caught on, and with his best baby talk blurted out, "Wuvoo Gampa," and smiled as he received a treat. This game was easy.

Six-year-old Adelaide, however, stubbornly refused. She wouldn't utter a word. She watched with jealousy and indignation as her brothers got treat after treat, but she still wouldn't budge. Soon the handful of treats were gone, and Adelaide burst into tears.

It was time for Grandma to intervene.

However, I didn't want to intervene in a way that undermined my husband, eliminated consequences, or rewarded petulance. So I gave Adelaide a hug and held up my hand for a high five. "High five Adelaide, you won. Good job! Did you like your prize?"

Confused, she pouted, "But I didn't get any prize."

"Oh, but you did. You won," I insisted. "You showed Grandpa that you're strong. You showed him that he can't make you do anything you don't want to do, and you succeeded. You won, and you got your prize for winning. If you say, 'I love you Grandpa,' then you win Grandpa's game, and get a treat for your prize; but if you don't say, 'I love you Grandpa,' you win a different game, and you get a different prize. Either way you win, and you get to choose which prize you get by which game you choose to play. So you won and got a prize. Did you like it?" I asked.

At this point, her father who was listening to the conversation added, "I've won lots of prizes like that."

"Me too," I smiled, "We all do that from time to time. We choose our prize, but sometimes the prizes aren't that great."

Adelaide, who is very bright, mulled over the idea. She looked for loopholes, and with each new idea of ways to circumnavigate Grandpa's game, I reaffirmed, "That's a great idea. If you do that, you totally win, and you'll get the prize you choose; but if you want to win Grandpa's game, and get a treat, then you just say the secret password, 'I love you Grandpa.' It's your choice. The prize you win is up to you."

"But I'm scared to say that," she complained.

"That's okay, sometimes it's scary to try something new and different, but I believe in you. I know you're strong," I reassured her.

Soon Grandpa reappeared with another handful of treats. "If you want a treat, you have to say the secret password, 'I love you Grandpa,'" he said playfully.

You could see the wheels turning in Adelaide's mind as she weighed her options. She hesitantly muttered, "I love you Grandpa." And was immediately rewarded with a treat.

"Good job Adelaide, you won a different game, and got a different prize. Did you like your prize this time?" I asked.

She smiled and nodded, then said more confidently, "I love you Grandpa." And got another treat. Between the three little ones, all chirping like little birds, the handful of treats quickly disappeared.

Choosing our reward

The story of Adelaide and the treats is a simple one, but the concept is universally applicable. We choose to do things because they bring us a reward of some kind. However, just like Adelaide who responded, "I didn't get any prize," we may not be aware of what we're doing, or the reward that we chose.

I have seen people willfully withhold forgiveness. They win because they refuse to let go of their anger and hatred. They win because they feel that they are champions of justice. They win because they believe that anger is strength, and forgiveness is weakness; but the reward is more anger, more hatred, more bitterness, a feeling of victimness, and a loss of peace and contentment. By choosing either to forgive or not forgive, we choose the prize associated with that decision. Either way we win, but the prizes are different.

I have seen people who refuse to forgive themselves. They win because they get to suffer, and they know that they deserve to suffer. They win because they believe that they are upholding justice. However, they miss out on the rewards of peace, contentment, and self-love.

I have seen people who will sacrifice anything to prove that they're right. They win because they prove that they are strong. They win because they know they are right, and being right is more important than anything else. They win because they keep their pride intact. They win because they know they are smarter than anybody else.

They win the prize of "rightness at all costs," but they may miss out on the prizes of relationships, cooperation, influence, peace, and happiness.

I have seen people stress themselves out with overwork and underappreciation. They win because they get to play the role of the martyr. They get to feel the righteous indignation of being overworked and underappreciated. They get the prize of self-righteousness and justified indignation. They get the prize of suffering and self-sacrifice. We can choose to play the role of a martyr, or we can choose a path that includes joy, peace, satisfaction, and being appreciated. Either way we win, but the prizes are different.

I have seen people who worry themselves sick. This is often evident in mothers who try to demonstrate their love through worry, fear, and self-sacrifice. They worry about their children. They worry about the choices they make. They worry about the future. They worry about everything, and they worry constantly. They win because they get to show their love and their self-sacrifice through the burdens they carry. They also play the role of the martyr. They win the prizes of suffering and self-sacrifice. We can choose this path, but when we do, we also choose the reward that comes with it.

Opening our hearts to a better way

Why do we choose these inferior rewards? Often it's because we aren't aware of what we're doing, or that we're making a choice at all. Many of us worry, stress, sacrifice, get angry, or withhold forgiveness because we're good people, and we believe we're fighting a good fight. We don't recognize that there might be another way, which is a better fight, that earns better rewards. If we want to reduce our fear, anxiety, worry, and stress, it is helpful and necessary to broaden our perspective and understanding.

We're going to do an exercise to help us recognize what our core beliefs are about fear, anxiety, worry, and stress, as well as any perceived rewards we receive. As we examine those core beliefs, we can then choose whether or not we want to modify those beliefs. As we examine our perceived rewards, we can choose whether or not we're willing to give up those perceived rewards for something better.

Journaling to find core beliefs and perceived rewards.

Using the answers to the questions from yesterday's journaling assignment, spend 20-30 minutes writing about one or more of the following prompts

- My core beliefs about fear, anxiety, worry, and stress are…

- Those core beliefs came from…

- My perceived rewards for fear, anxiety, worry, and stress are…

Day 10 - Visualization to let go of unnecessary burdens

We've been actively looking for ways to reduce stressors. We've done exercises to help us to identify and evaluate our core beliefs, and to determine any perceived rewards from carrying excess fear, anxiety, worry, and stress. Hopefully by this point, with an increased awareness, we can see that at least some of our burdens are unnecessary, and we are willing to let go of some of that excess. Today's action step is a visualization technique designed to help us let go of unnecessary burdens.

Research shows that visualization and imagery techniques are helpful therapies to facilitate healing.[168] We're also going to include an element that has proven effective to innumerable hosts of people who have healed from addictions by following 12 step addiction recovery programs, and that is calling on a higher power.[169]

The main benefit of using the words *higher power* is that it cannot be easily defined, and people can interpret the concept as they wish. Most people interpret *higher power* as meaning a god, but it does not have to be interpreted this way. It is left up to the individual to decide how they wish to define it. It could be God, or the Universe, or karma, or whatever feels comfortable for you. There are no rules except that this power has to be greater than the individual.[170] This makes it possible for a Christian, a Buddhist, or even an atheist to work side by side to tap into the scientifically verified benefits of spirituality on physical, mental, and emotional well-being. A large volume of research shows that people who are more religious/spiritual have better mental health and adapt more quickly to health problems compared to those who are less religious/spiritual.[171]

When people believe in a power greater than themselves, it can facilitate healing and make life easier. For example, when a person feels overwhelmed by a task, and may not believe that they have the ability to defeat their problem alone, relying on a power greater than themselves can help give them the strength they need. When people believe in a higher power, they will usually find it easier to forgive other people who have wronged them. It also becomes much easier to let go of resentments. Furthermore, as a person faces challenges, it can be a great source of comfort to believe in a higher power that is providing them with help. If a challenge becomes overwhelming, a person can hand it over to their higher power. This can be like lifting a great weight off their shoulders. When people develop the ability to let go, it brings them peace of mind and contentment. Belief in a higher power can also give people a sense of purpose and meaning in their life.

Visualization exercise

The visualization exercise for today is to symbolically hand over our emotional burdens to our higher power. During this visualization, I'm going to use the pronouns "he and his" when referring to the higher power, but you could substitute the pronouns "she and her," or "it and its," if that feels more appropriate to you.

Take a few deep, belly breaths and close your eyes to minimize distractions. I want you to visualize that you are hiking up a mountain trail. I want you to look around and notice as much detail as you can. What does the scenery look like? What kinds of trees do you see? Is the path steep, or is it a gentle incline? Is the sun shining, or is it stormy? Notice the time of day and the season. Notice any smells that might be there. Notice any sounds that you might hear. Notice your position on the trail; are you just starting at the bottom of the trail, nearing the top, or somewhere in the middle?

As you're walking along, you notice that something seems to be hampering your progress. Then you notice that you're carrying a bag, and inside this bag are rocks that symbolize your emotional burdens.

Now I want you to pay attention to the bag you are carrying. What kind of bag is it? Is it a backpack, or maybe a big sack like a pillowcase that you hold onto with your hand as it swings over one shoulder? What does it look like? Imagine the color, texture, and feel of the bag. What is it made out of? How big is it? How heavy is it? Is it nearly empty or bulging, stretching, and ready to burst the seams?

Now imagine the rocks inside the bag that represent those hurtful emotions that you're carrying. It might include feelings of fear, anxiety, worry, stress, anger, resentment, shame, abandonment, or betrayal. Or it might include something else that concerns a current situation, or perhaps an event that happened in the past, or even an anticipated event in the future. What do these rocks look like? What type of stone are they? Are they smooth, or are they jagged? Describe the size, color, and shape of the rocks. How do you feel as you heft their weight in your bag? Is it easy, or are your legs buckling under the weight?

Now, pay attention to your pace as you continue up the trail. Are you running, skipping, walking, trudging, stumbling, or even crawling? How do you feel?

As you're traveling along the path, you turn and notice that someone is traveling beside you. Although you've never met this personage before, you recognize that it is your higher power. What does he look like? What does it feel like to be in his presence?

Your higher power has the ability to see through your bag, and is aware of each and every emotional burden you are carrying, as well as all the circumstances and events that caused them. He looks at you with compassion and empathy.

Now you feel an overwhelming sense of love and acceptance sweeping over you. This love is deep and intense. You feel it from the tip of your toes to the crown of your head. You accept this love and allow it to flow through you. You know, without a doubt, and perhaps for the first time, that your higher power cares deeply, personally, and intimately about you.

Your higher power calls you by name and offers to take your burdens. He is all powerful, and these burdens are light to him; in fact, he considers it a pleasure to be able to serve you. However, he will not force you against your will, because he respects you too much to take away your agency.

What happens next? Do you accept his offer? Do you give him the whole bag, or do you sort through it and select just a few stones from inside the bag, and hand him those while choosing to keep the rest? What thoughts and feelings are going through your mind as you hand him the stones?

Whether you were willing to let go of all, some, or none of your stones, you see your higher power smile at you; and once again you feel that overwhelming feeling of love sweeping over you. He loves you if you keep your stones, and he loves you if you let them go. He honors your freedom to choose.

What happens next? What message does your higher power want to share with you? What encouragement does he give? What advice does he give?

It's time for him to go now, but your higher power is willing to come again and walk beside you. He's also willing to ease your burdens if you ask, believe that he'll take them, and be willing to let them go.

Notice your surroundings again. Pay attention to any changes that may have occurred. Is your bag any lighter? Does it take less effort as you hike up the trail? Notice your pace as you continue along the trail. Are you running, skipping, walking, trudging, stumbling, or even crawling? Is it any different from before? How do you feel?

Look around at the scenery; is it the same or has it changed as well? Look around and notice as much detail as you can. What kinds of trees do you see? Is the path steep or is it a gentle incline? Is the sun shining or is it stormy? Notice the quality of the light. Notice the time of day and the season. Notice any smells that might be there. Notice any sounds that you might hear.

Now it's time for you to return as well, but remember that you can return here any time that you want to. I want you to return your focus to your breathing. Take a few more breaths while you allow the vision to slowly fade, and you return to your natural surroundings.

Day 11 - Connect with nature and/or exercise

Today's action step is to spend 30 minutes connecting with nature and/or exercising. If you need a reminder of what to do, or why to do it, please review the information for day 2.

Day 12 - Core beliefs about self-worth and lovability

Today's action step is a journaling exercise to become more aware of our core beliefs about our self-worth and lovability (am I worthy of being loved?)

The value of a human soul

How is self-worth determined? Many of us use external factors like: wealth, status, accomplishments, popularity, or other people's opinions to determine whether or not we have value, and whether or not we are lovable/likable. However, the truth is that the value of a human soul is intrinsic. Intrinsic means "belonging to a thing by its very nature."[172] It comes from the Latin word *intrinsecus* which means interior or inner. Some synonyms for intrinsic include: inherent, innate, inborn, natural, built-in, inseparable, permanent, indelible, ineradicable, integral, and fundamental.[173]

Let me repeat, the value of a human soul is intrinsic; it comes from the inside. You have infinite worth simply because you exist. It is your birthright. It doesn't need to be earned or verified, and it is completely independent of any external factors. Deep down inside, you know that already. There are a few moments in the lifespan of a person that we reflexively respond to that knowledge. One is when a baby is born. The love that parents feel for their infant child is beyond their ability to express. Does that baby have value and worth? Oh yes! Is that baby lovable/likable? Oh yes! What did the baby do to earn that worth and that lovability? Absolutely nothing. They possess those qualities simply by existing. Do those qualities of worth and lovability diminish over time? No.

Another moment in time where we are reminded of the intrinsic value of a human soul, is when a life is taken, and we mourn the loss of someone we care about. Furthermore, the laws of the land reserve the harshest punishments for those who take another person's life by force. In the courtroom, they do not examine the victim's wealth, status, accomplishments or popularity in order to evaluate the worth of that person and determine the punishment of the offender. A life is a life, and each life has intrinsic value. Our worth and value are inborn, natural, built-in, inseparable, and permanent.

What we believe matters more than what is true

We have intrinsic value, that's a fact, but just because something is true doesn't mean we believe it. Recall our discussions about the mere exposure effect which says that we tend to believe things that we hear over and over again, simply because of the repetition, and not because it is actually true. Even though we have inherent worth and lovability as our birthright, we may have been told by others, or even by ourselves, so many times that we're worthless, or that we have to do something to earn and prove our value and lovability that we believe it. And in this case, what we believe is more important than what is actually true.

Researcher Brene Brown came to a similar conclusion after her six-year study on what causes shame.[174] She wanted to know why some people enjoy love and belonging while others are always wondering if they're good enough. She found that it all comes down to one single variable: a person's belief of whether or not they're worthy.

> *"There was only one variable that separated the people who have a strong sense of love and belonging and the people who really struggle for it. And that was, the people who have a strong sense of love and belonging believe they're worthy of love and belonging. That's it. They believe they're worthy... [T]he one thing that keeps us out of connection is our fear that we're not worthy of connection..."*
>
> - *Brene Brown*

Journaling on lovability

Today's action step is to increase awareness about your perception of your lovability and self-worth by looking deeper at your core values and beliefs. Spend 20-30 minutes writing on one or more of the following prompts:

- I have inherent value and lovability because…

- I believe I only have worth and value if …

- I believe I am only lovable if…

- My beliefs about my value and lovability came from…

Day 13 - Evaluating threats to lovability

Today's action step is to evaluate stressors that are perceived as threats to our self-worth and lovability.

We've had an opportunity to become more aware of the connections between our thoughts, emotions and behaviors by looking at the CBT triangle. We've discussed cognitive distortions that may pop up in our automatic thoughts. We've done some journaling to dig deeper and become aware of our core beliefs that may fuel those dysfunctional automatic thoughts. We've looked into our own core beliefs about self-worth and lovability. Today we're going to dig a little bit deeper. It's interesting to note that according to cognitive behavioral scientists, if we keep digging deep enough, we nearly always come to the same basic questions: Am I lovable? Am I worthy of love and belonging? Am I good enough?

Here's an example. Bob is stressed and upset about the way someone treated him, and it's eating at him, and he just can't let it go. He's sharing his frustrations with his friend Tom, who helps him use a downward arrow to dig deeper, and try to find the source of the problem.

Bob: This guy at work showed blatant disrespect for me, by doing _____ and I'm so angry. I want to get back at him somehow, and I just can't seem to let it go.

Tom: What makes you feel like you need to "get back at him"?

Bob: There should be a consequence when someone does something wrong. That's justice. I can't just let him get away with it.

Tom: What does it mean if you let someone get away with disrespecting you?

Bob: It sets me up for me to be abused again. It shows that I'm weak.

Tom: What does it mean if you're weak?

Bob: It means that I'm a loser, and that no one likes me.

In this example, Bob is upset about an action that he felt was disrespectful. When you try to dig deeper, Bob is certain that his core beliefs about justice are what is driving him to want revenge, or at least a consequence of some kind for the person that offended him. He has strong feelings about right and wrong, and he wants to see justice served; but if you dig even deeper you find that Bob is trying to protect the very essence of himself: his value, his worth, and his lovability.

Recall from our earlier discussions that fear-based emotions are intended to keep us safe by heightening awareness and improving performance. They are part of a system designed to protect us from harm. We want to protect our physical bodies from harm, and we also want to protect the very essence of who we are: our value, our worth, and our likability/lovability. Fear-based emotions can arise when we feel a threat to either of these aspects of self, which I'm going to call our physical safety and our self-worth safety.

Think of a stressful event. List any thoughts and emotions related to that event. Then evaluate whether you believe that these thoughts and fear based emotions are based on real or perceived threats to your physical safety (P) or your self-worth safety (S).

Threat evaluation chart

Emotions	P or S	Thoughts	P or S

Looking at the three stories from the introduction, we can find several examples of this. In the story of Lewis flying up the canyon, obviously he felt fear because his physical safety was threatened. But if you pay close attention, there is another time that he felt his self-worth was being threatened when his friend Ron seemed unimpressed with Lewis' flying skills, and it wounded his pride. Because Lewis' feelings of self-worth and likability were tightly intertwined with his identity as a pilot, he interpreted this as an attack on his very being. To protect his self-worth, he began to show off, which led to making a really stupid decision that severely threatened their physical safety.

Flying up the canyon

Emotions	P or S	Thoughts	P or S
Pride	S	I want Ron to be impressed	S
Fear, worry, stress, anxiety, terror, panic	P	We're going to die	P

In the story of the dreaded phone calls, I feared that rejection was evidence that I wasn't lovable or valued. Avoiding the phone calls was a way to protect myself from that threat to my self-worth.

Dreaded phone calls

Emotions	P or S	Thoughts	P or S
Fear, worry, stress, anxiety, dread, guilt	S	I don't want to do this,	S
		They're going to reject me,	S
		Nobody likes me,	S
		I don't know what to say	S

In the story about our granola days of poverty, we feared for both physical safety and self-worth safety. We feared about the ability to take care of our physical needs like food and a place to live, but we also feared about how this reflected on our self-worth. Money and success are common methods we use to determine our self-worth, and we didn't have either. Comparing our situation to that of the neighbor, who happened to be a teenage mom on welfare, dropped our feelings of self-worth to an all-time low.

Granola days/poverty - can't afford rent

Emotions	P or S	Thoughts	P or S
Fear, worry, stress, anxiety, shame, panic, discouraged, depressed, hopeless	P, S	How are we going to pay the rent?	P
		I'm embarrassed that we're so poor.	S
		We're worse off than a teenage mom on welfare.	S
		We're never going to be successful	P

Fear-based emotions of fear, anxiety, worry, and stress can arise when we feel a threat to either our physical safety or our self-worth safety. We often try to protect our self-worth by avoiding situations where we might feel threatened, or we may respond inappropriately when we feel that our self-worth is being threatened, but there is a better way.

Reducing fear by accepting truth

If we accept the truth that we have inherent worth and lovability, then it can reduce our fear-based feelings dramatically. Remember that fear-based emotions are intended to keep us safe by heightening awareness and improving performance. They are part of a system designed to protect us from harm. We want to protect our physical bodies from harm, and we also want to protect the very essence of who we are: our value, our worth, and our likability or lovability. Fear-based emotions can arise when we feel a threat to either of these aspects. If we come to realize that the value of a human soul is intrinsic, inherent, innate, inborn, natural, built-in, inseparable, permanent, indelible, ineradicable, integral, and fundamental, then we recognize that nothing can truly threaten our self-worth. Threats to our self-worth are perceived threats. While it's true that our reputation, our popularity, other people's opinions, and even our own perception of our value and lovability can change for the better, or for the worse, nothing can actually diminish your built-in and very permanent inherent value. It is a part of you. You were born with inherent value, and you get to keep it.

One of the reasons that I ask you to spend two minutes looking and pondering about the "I am" chart as part of each morning and evening routine, is to reawaken your awareness that you have inherent worth and value. It comes from the inside. If we strengthen our belief in these basic truths, then our burdens become more manageable and life becomes happier.

The action step for today is to evaluate the sources of threat for a particular event. What was the event? What were your emotions? What were your thoughts? If possible, try to include thoughts about self, about others, and about the world in general.

Evaluate any emotions you may have experienced like fear, anxiety, worry, and/or stress. Remember that fear based emotions can arise when we feel a real or perceived threat to either our physical safety or our self-worth safety. Next to each emotion listed on the chart, write the letters P or S to represent whether you think this was a threat to your physical safety or your self-worth safety.

Evaluate any thoughts you may have experienced whether about yourself, others, or the world around you. Write the letters P or S next to any thoughts that might relate to your physical safety or your self-worth safety.

Something to think about: Would any of those emotions or thoughts be different if you had a firm and unshakable belief in your own inherent value?

Day 14 - Connect with nature and/or exercise

Today's action step is to spend 30 minutes connecting with nature and/or exercising. If you need a reminder of what to do, or why to do it, please review the information for day 2.

Day 15 – Practicing alternate methods of showing love and concern

We're always looking for ways to reduce fear, anxiety, worry, and stress, and today's objective is to see if we might be carrying any unnecessary burdens relating to other people. Remember that on a primal level, fear-based emotions are intended to keep us safe by heightening awareness and improving performance. Sometimes we misinterpret this and conclude that the emotions of fear, anxiety, or worry are actually what is keeping us and our loved ones safe. If we worry hard enough, then the bad thing won't actually happen. This simply isn't true.

Some ways we might carry the burdens of others is worrying about the people we care about. Parents are often guilty of this. On some level, they believe that if they worry enough about their children, then it will keep them safe. Even though chronic worry can cause a host of mental, emotional, and physical problems, a parent who believes that worrying will keep his or her children safe will not allow himself or herself to give up worrying. They do it because they are willing to sacrifice their own health and wellbeing to protect their children, and this often continues long after the children have grown to adulthood.

Some people believe that fear, anxiety, and worry are expressions of love. If I care about someone, then I worry about them. Therefore, the more I worry, the greater my expression of love. Again, even though chronic worrying can ruin a person's life, they continue to do it because they are willing to sacrifice themselves for the people they love.

Although these deep seated beliefs have good and noble intentions, it doesn't actually work that way. Chronic fear, anxiety, and/or worry do not protect us, or the people we care about. Instead it harms us mentally, emotionally, and physically, and can damage relationships with the people we care about.

Some of you might be thinking, "But I can't stop worrying. What if they make mistakes? What if they get hurt? What if [fill in the blank]?" I can't guarantee that the "what ifs" won't happen if you choose to let go of worry. But I can't guarantee that they won't happen when you're consumed with worry either. Life happens, and sometimes life is messy, but worrying about it does not make it better or easier.

Alternate ways to show love and concern

Let's discuss some alternate ways to show love and support for the people we care about.

First of all, let's clarify a little more about what worrying is. Worry is concern coupled with fear. It is possible to care about someone, and to be concerned about them, without adding fear into the mix. We can be concerned about someone who is experiencing hardships, but add love and trust to that concern rather than fear.

Trusting people to be able to make their own choices and to be able to handle their own problems empowers them. Worrying about people weakens them, because it shows that you don't have confidence in their ability to cope. Trusting them shows that you believe in them.

But what if it's hard, or they get hurt, or they make a mistake, or make a bad decision that leads to unpleasant consequences? Our loved ones will most likely face all kinds of challenges. That is a part of life. We all face challenges. But when that happens, we can have confidence that their experiences, whether good or bad, are perfect for them. I'm going to say that again. Our experiences are perfect *for us.* They are tailor made to provide us with the experiences and lessons that we need to become our best selves.

We learn strength, empathy, and wisdom from our mistakes. We don't always learn from our mistakes the first time, but then we tend to make that same mistake again until we do learn. Most of us are kinetic learners; we learn best by doing and experiencing things for ourselves. If we're smart, we can also learn from the mistakes of other people. Trust your loved ones to be able to handle their own problems, trust that their experiences are perfect *for them.* Show that you believe in them, and that you honor and respect their agency.

What if they come to you and expect you to solve their problems for them? Let them know that you love them, and trust them to be able to solve their own problems. You might say something like, "What are you going to do about it?" rather than immediately jumping in to provide solutions. Show them that you have confidence that they are stronger than they realize. Loving someone does not mean that you are required to solve their problems for them. Loving someone does not mean that you need to remove their consequences either. That doesn't mean that we don't help and support them, it just means that we don't accept the responsibility for their problems.

Playing a supporting role

You are the star of your own life story, the center of your universe, but you only play a supporting role in the lives of other people. You carry the burden of responsibility for your own problems, but you don't need to carry the burden of someone else's. In fact, you really can't, even if you try.

I understand that this is difficult for many people. I know people who *want* to show their love through their self-sacrifice, and they're used to playing the role of the martyr. They may prefer the feelings of suffering and self-sacrifice that go along with the perceived control of worrying. They may find those feelings and rewards more satisfying than the rewards of joy, peace, confidence, and contentment that accompany letting go and trusting people to make their own choices. And that's okay. I respect your agency. Whatever you choose will be perfect for you, and you're welcome to change your mind at any time.

Today's action step is practicing an alternate response to worrying about the people we care about. It is a variation of the loving-kindness meditation that is part of the morning routine. Rather than sending worry out into the universe, we're going to send loving-kindness to someone we care about, and then to ourselves.

Loving-kindness meditation II

To begin, sit upright in a comfortable chair with both feet flat on the floor and your hands resting gently in your lap. Close your eyes to minimize distractions and take a few deep, belly breaths. Just relax and focus on the gentle sensation of breathing in and out.

Now I want you to pick an image of a person, just a mental image of someone you care about; it can be whoever you like and just imagine you're looking at that person. While you're focusing on that image we're going to say a simple mantra, and I want you to imagine that you're saying it to that person.

"I care about you. I have confidence in you. I trust that you have the strength and wisdom to handle your challenges. I trust that your experiences will be perfect for you. I respect your agency, and I love you without reservation. May you be safe and happy."

"I care about you. I have confidence in you. I trust that you have the strength and wisdom to handle your challenges. I trust that your

experiences will be perfect for you. I respect your agency, and I love you without reservation. May you be safe and happy."

"I care about you. I have confidence in you. I trust that you have the strength and wisdom to handle your challenges. I trust that your experiences will be perfect for you. I respect your agency, and I love you without reservation. May you be safe and happy."

Now I'd like you to change the image, and I want you to imagine you're looking in a mirror. So you're looking at yourself as you repeat this mantra. This is a message for you.

"I care about you. I have confidence in you. I trust that you have the strength and wisdom to handle your challenges. I trust that your experiences will be perfect for you. I respect your agency, and I love you without reservation. May you be safe and happy."

"I care about you. I have confidence in you. I trust that you have the strength and wisdom to handle your challenges. I trust that your experiences will be perfect for you. I respect your agency, and I love you without reservation. May you be safe and happy."

"I care about you. I have confidence in you. I trust that you have the strength and wisdom to handle your challenges. I trust that your experiences will be perfect for you. I respect your agency, and I love you without reservation. May you be safe and happy."

Bring your attention back to your breath. Take a few more deep breaths, then gently open your eyes.

Creating a virtual shield

Another alternative to worrying is to create a virtual shield around the people that you care about. Worrying is basically trying to protect our loved ones with our thoughts. Creating a virtual shield for your loved ones is the same principle, but without fostering fear or causing self-damage in the process.

To begin, sit upright in a comfortable chair with both feet flat on the floor and your hands resting gently in your lap. Close your eyes to minimize distractions, and take a few deep, belly breaths. Just relax and focus on the gentle sensation of breathing in and out.

Imagine, intend, and visualize creating a shield or force field that completely surrounds your loved ones. Be creative and specific in imagining what it looks like, what color it is, how it feels inside. Notice the quality of the light and any other specific details you can think of. Fill the space inside this shield or force field with love, confidence, hope, and peace. Imagine your loved one being enveloped with feelings of love and peace. Imagine that this shield is a protection for your loved one. They are safe. The shield is a filter, not a wall. Only those experiences that will be for your loved one's greater good can enter through this filter. Only those experiences that are perfect for them are allowed to enter. Everything is going to be okay. In the end, everything is going to be okay. Your loved one is surrounded and protected by love, and empowered by your trust and confidence in him or her.

Bring your attention back to your breath. Take a few more deep breaths, then gently open your eyes.

Day 16 - Finding meaning and purpose

We've discussed many different tools and techniques to become aware of any stressors that might be reduced, or even eliminated, by increasing awareness and altering perspective. However, there are many stressors that cannot be eliminated. The purpose of today's action step is to strengthen and empower us to be able to better deal with those problems that we cannot change, by becoming aware of our values, meaning, and purpose.

Meaning brings purpose

In 1942, a prominent Jewish psychologist living in Vienna had a serious problem that he was powerless to change. Victor Frankl was arrested and sent to a Nazi concentration camp. His pregnant wife, parents, and extended family were also arrested and sent to other camps.[175]

He immediately noticed that some prisoners gave up right away while others continued to struggle and survive even long after they rightfully should have died considering their malnourishment and sustained injuries. With a mind trained in psychology, he couldn't help but ask *why,* and he quickly understood that it had a lot to do with attitude. He wrote, *"Everything can be taken from a man but one thing: the last of the human freedoms — to choose one's attitude in any given set of circumstances, to choose one's own way."*

Based on his own experience and the experiences of those around him, Frankl argues that we cannot avoid suffering, but we can choose how to cope with it, find meaning in it, and move forward with renewed purpose. He wrote, *"Life has a meaning to the very last breath... the possibility of realizing values by the very attitude with which we face our destined suffering... exists to the very last moment... He who has a 'why' to live can bear with almost any 'how'."*[176]

> *"He who has a 'why' to live can bear with almost any 'how'."*
>
> ~ *Victor Frankl*

Frankl's personal experiences gave him an opportunity to put his own theories to the ultimate test. While he was enduring the hardships of the concentration camps, Frankl's "why" to live was his family. He needed to survive so he could be reunited with his wife, and the other members of his family. He imagined his wife as a light in the darkness. He bolstered his attitude by actively looking for small joys like a sunrise, a bird singing, or the view of a farmhouse in the distance.

When the horrors of the concentration camp finally ended in 1945, and he returned home to Vienna, he learned that his wife and all of his family members, except for one sister, were dead. His meaning was gone. But then he did something extraordinary, he found new meaning. His meaning became sharing the importance of meaning with the world. His book *Man's Search for Meaning* is considered to be one of the top ten most influential books of all time.[177]

Meaning is something we construct

So how do we find meaning? A quote from John Gardner, an American novelist, essayist, and university professor, helps clarify how we find meaning.[178] He said, *"Meaning is not something you stumble across, like the answer to a riddle or the prize in a treasure hunt. Meaning is something you build into your life. You build it out of your own past, out of your affection and loyalties... out of your own talent and understanding, out of the things you believe in, out of the things and people you love, out of the values for which you are willing to sacrifice something.*[79]

Values clarification chart

We get to choose how and where we find our meaning. We have values and priorities. We have things that bring joy and satisfaction, but sometimes we lose sight of these things. Today's assignment is to fill out a values clarification chart. The chart has four columns. The first lists a few common values. The next column is labeled "Importance." In this column rate how important each of these values is to you, on a scale from 1-10. The next column is labeled "Time/resources." In this column, again using a scale from 1-10, rate how much time, energy, and resources you devote to this value. The last column is labeled "Difference." In this column subtract the number in the "Time/resources" column from the number in the "Importance" column. Look for those areas where there is a significant difference between the things that you value, and the amount of time, energy, and resources you are devoting to those values. We can increase feelings of meaning and purpose in our lives by spending our time, energy, and resources on those things that we value most.

Sample chart for Jill

Values	Importance	Time/ resources	Difference
Marriage/intimate relationship	10	5	5
Parenting	10	9	1

Family	10	7	3
Social/friendships	5	3	2
Career	8	8	0
Education/growth	3	1	2
Relaxation	3	1	2
Spirituality	8	3	5
Citizenship/causes	3	2	1
Health	8	4	4
Other: service	7	4	3

In the sample chart, it looks like Jill might find more meaning in her life if she invested more time and energy in nurturing her marriage, and in developing her spirituality, because these are things that she values, but isn't spending a proportionate amount of time and energy caring for those things. She also might want to look at things she can do to maintain her health. Our values change during different phases of our lives, and as circumstances change. Feel free to re-evaluate your values by filling in a fresh chart whenever you choose.

Day 17 – Finding meaning and purpose part 2

Yesterday's assignment was to complete a value's clarification chart and notice if there are any things that you value, but aren't spending a proportionate amount of time, energy, and resources nurturing that value. Today's action step is a follow up from that assignment. Spend 30 minutes doing something that brings meaning into your life. Something that you value. It might be going on a date with your romantic partner, playing with your kids, calling a friend, going to the gym, service, praying and meditating, or anything that brings meaning and purpose into your life.

18 - Finding joy

The action step for today is to remember and reawaken those activities that bring you joy. Often, when people are struggling with feelings of being overwhelmed with fear, anxiety, worry, and/or stress, they eliminate things from their lives that bring them joy. They feel that there's too much to do, and there just isn't enough time, or they're just not in the mood. However, experts say that positive emotions can decrease stress hormones, build emotional strength, and improve resilience.

Laughter

Research shows that laughing can decrease pain, promote muscle relaxation, and help reduce anxiety. It helps you shift perspective, allowing you to see situations in a more realistic, less threatening light.[180]

Laughter makes you feel good. It triggers the release of endorphins, the body's natural feel-good chemicals. And the good feeling that you get when you laugh remains with you even after the laughter subsides. Humor helps you keep a positive, optimistic outlook through difficult situations, disappointments, and loss. It adds joy and zest to life, eases anxiety and tension, relieves stress, improves mood, and strengthens resilience.

Hobbies/leisure activities

Doing things that you enjoy is a natural way to relieve stress and find your happy place. Leisure activities disrupt the cycle of stress. When we're stressed out, we tend to get a sort of tunnel vision, where we can only see our problems; but if we allow ourselves to take a break, then we can broaden our perspective and see things from a fresh point of view. This makes it easier to find creative solutions to our problems.[182, 183]

Journaling - activities and core beliefs about joy

Today's action step is a journaling exercise. What brings you joy? First, list as many things as you can think of that bring you joy, or have brought you joy in the past. For example: scrapbooking, painting, playing a musical instrument, sewing, knitting, sports, yoga, meeting a friend for lunch, reading, writing, walking, cycling, making jewelry, sketching, writing poetry, working in the garden, etc.

Second, think about your core beliefs about joy, recreation, leisure, and laughter. Do you allow yourself to do those things, or are there beliefs that you're supposed to outgrow these activities, or perhaps they're a waste of time, and you're supposed to be doing more productive things?

Please spend 20-30 minutes journaling on one or more of the following prompts:

- Things that bring me joy…

- What kinds of activities did I used to find enjoyable, but haven't done for a while?

- My core beliefs about hobbies and leisure activities are…

- I learned these beliefs from…

Day - 19 Finding Joy part 2

Today's action step is a continuation from yesterday's assignment. Spend 30 minutes doing something that brings you joy.

Day - 20 Gratitude

Today's action step is designed to harness the power of a grateful attitude in overcoming feelings of fear, anxiety, worry, and stress. Much research has been done on the effects of gratitude on the body and mind; and they indicate that gratitude builds resilience, and is a powerfully effective tool to help us deal with stressors. Studies show that gratitude increases feelings of happiness and optimism, builds confidence, and alleviates social anxiety. It has even been shown to lower systolic blood pressure, to decrease cortisol, and can actually rewire the brain.[184, 185, 186, 187, 188]

A fascinating study on the effects of gratitude was performed at Berkeley University; they divided participants into a control group and an experimental group that actively practiced daily gratitude.[189] Using a fMRI scanner, they measured the brain activity of the study participants. They found that those who practiced gratitude showed greater activity in the medial prefrontal cortex region of the brain compared to those in the control group. The prefrontal cortex is a brain area associated with learning and decision making. This would imply that cultivating an attitude of gratitude can help us make better decisions. Our brains seem to function better when we are grateful.[190] Furthermore, additional studies indicate that gratitude improves brain neuroplasticity; which, in simple terms, means that it improves your brain's ability to adapt to change.[191, 192]

Gratitude journaling

Gratitude provides benefits on physical, emotional, and mental levels. It lifts the weight of anxiety off our shoulders, and we can see the good, even when we're facing difficult situations. It reduces stress hormone levels, and also improves brain function and elasticity, which helps us be able to calm down, think better, and be able to adapt to change.

It helps us be happier, more optimistic, more resilient, and builds confidence. In short, gratitude is good for us. Today's action step is to list 100 things that you're grateful for.

Day 21 - The healing power of forgiveness

Today we're going to look at how the concept of forgiveness might be able to reduce our mental and emotional burdens. The action step will be a journaling exercise to increase awareness of your core beliefs about forgiveness.

Forgiveness is a concept that is often misunderstood. Some people believe that in order to forgive someone you have to be able to say, "That's okay," and somehow minimize or absolve the offender for their actions against you. But often the offender's actions were not "okay," and no amount of passage of time will make it "okay." This assumption often leads a person to think that forgiveness violates justice.

Earlier we discussed how our emotions serve a purpose, but that purpose can be misconstrued. We talked about the concept that fear based emotions are intended to keep us safe by heightening awareness and improving performance, but sometimes we misinterpret this and conclude that the emotions of fear, anxiety, or worry are actually what is keeping us safe. We are therefore reluctant to let those feelings go as long as we believe they are necessary for our safety. Similarly, we are reluctant to forgive others if we feel that withholding forgiveness is necessary to uphold justice and fairness.

Let's delve a little deeper into the concept of forgiveness, so that you may make a better informed decision on whether or not to withhold forgiveness.

First, let's clarify what forgiveness is *not*. Experts who study or teach forgiveness make it clear that forgiveness is not excusing or condoning either a person or their action. Forgiveness is not surrendering, and does not imply weakness. Forgiveness is not resignation or passivity. Forgiveness does not indicate a balancing of the scales or that justice has been satisfied. Forgiving someone doesn't obligate you to reconcile with the person who harmed you, or release them from legal accountability.[193]

Psychologists generally define forgiveness as a conscious, deliberate decision to release feelings of resentment or vengeance toward a person or group who has harmed you, regardless of whether or not they actually deserve your forgiveness.[194] Forgiveness doesn't mean that you have to forget the incident, but it implies that you are able to detach the negative feelings associated with the event.

Although forgiveness does benefit the person who is being forgiven, the primary benefactor is actually the person who is doing the forgiving. Forgiveness brings the forgiver peace of mind, and frees him or her from corrosive anger and deeply held negative feelings. In that way, it empowers you to recognize the pain you suffered without letting that pain define you, and enables you to heal and move on with your life.

Furthermore, forgiveness also benefits us physically. Research shows that the act of forgiveness can improve the quality of our sleep, reduce pain, lower the risk of heart attack, improve cholesterol levels, reduce blood pressure and levels of anxiety, depression, and stress.[195]

On the other hand, holding a grudge can harm you emotionally, mentally, and physically. A study from Emory University found that bitter people had higher blood pressure, and were more likely to die from heart disease than more forgiving people.[196] Research shows that holding a grudge increases stress by boosting cortisol levels, and decreases happiness by diminishing oxytocin. In addition, prolonged feelings of resentment can also negatively impact metabolism, immune response, and organ function. It keeps your body locked in that fight or flight response which leads to a variety of chronic diseases.[197]

One of my favorite examples demonstrating the personal benefits of forgiveness is the story of Corrie Ten Boom, which she shares in her book *The Hiding Place*.[199] Corrie was a middle aged Dutch watchmaker happily living a content and quiet life with her father and sister Betsie, when their lives were forever altered by the horrors of the Holocaust during World War II. This devout Christian family joined the underground, and helped many Jews escape the Nazis by hiding them in their home. Eventually they were caught and arrested. She endured the privation and degradation of Ravensbruck concentration camp. Before the war ended, both her father and her sister died.

When Corrie was released from prison, she set up a rehabilitation center in the Netherlands to help others, like herself, who had been prisoners or war. She found it interesting that it was not the Germans or the Japanese that these people had the hardest time forgiving; it was their fellow Dutchmen who had sided with the enemy. But in every case, forgiveness played an integral part of the healing process.[200]

She scheduled speaking engagements, and wherever she went, she spoke of the healing power of forgiveness. After one of these speeches in Germany, she was startled to have a man that she recognized as a former guard at Ravensbruck come up to her, and thank her for her message. It was the first time since her release that she had stood face to face with one of her captors, and her blood seemed to freeze. Suddenly forgiveness wasn't a general concept; it was personal and specific.

The man thrust out his hand to shake hers, but she felt momentarily paralyzed. Although she hesitated, and struggled with her emotions for a moment, she prayed for divine strength, and allowed herself to raise her hand woodenly and mechanically. Then she says an amazing thing took place. She describes a feeling like a current starting at her shoulder and racing down her arm into their joined hands, and into her heart sprang a mercy and charity towards this former enemy that almost overwhelmed her.[201]

The story of Corrie Ten Boom illustrates the truthfulness in the concept that although forgiveness can benefit the one being forgiven, the primary benefit goes to the one doing the forgiving. Forgiveness is about healing the soul of the person who was hurt.

Today's action step is a journaling exercise to increase awareness of your core beliefs about forgiveness, or to do a visualization exercise. Spend 20-30 minutes writing about one or more of the following prompts:

- If I forgive someone, that means…

- I don't want to forgive others because…

- I don't want to forgive myself because...

- Forgiving others or myself might reduce my stress because…

- I used to think forgiveness meant…, but now I believe forgiveness means...

Alternate activity - self forgiveness visualization exercise

Sometimes a person is willing to forgive others, but is unwilling to forgive themselves. They feel like they deserve to suffer, and forgiving themselves would be unjust. The same principles apply to forgiving yourself as forgiving other people. Remember that psychologists generally define forgiveness as a conscious, deliberate decision to release feelings of resentment or vengeance toward a person whether or not they actually deserve your forgiveness. An alternate activity to the journaling exercise is to visualize yourself in a scenario, similar to the one described by Corrie Ten Boom when she met her former guard, only this time it is you facing yourself in the mirror. You know your past, just like Corrie knew the guard's past. Will you choose to lift your hand and touch the hand in the mirror?

Day 22 - Relationship stress

Relationships and interactions with other people can be sources of stress. Today's action step, called a virtual conversation, is a coping tool to reduce stress in dealing with other people.

Why we're doing this exercise

Recall the journaling exercise that we did on day one. The purpose was to relieve burdens by writing them down. We related feelings of being overwhelmed by stress and burdens to the image of an over-inflated balloon; you can see the strain on the surface and know that it will explode at the slightest provocation. However, if some of the pressure is released from the balloon, it becomes much more pliable and resilient.

The virtual conversation has a similar purpose. It is intended to relieve stress by allowing ourselves to feel our feelings, and say what we want to say, in an environment that is safe and won't exacerbate the problem. A virtual conversation can also bring healing and closure.

Have you ever had the experience where someone says something insulting to you and hours later you think of the perfect response that you wish you had said? Or you hold your true feelings inside because you don't want to get into an argument? Are there things you wish you could say, but you're trying to be polite? Most of us use a personal filter when we speak to people. We might share some of what we're thinking or feeling, but we hold a lot back. A virtual conversation is your chance to say the rest of what you're feeling. You don't hold anything back. You put it all on the table.

A virtual conversation is similar to some of the other visualization techniques we've tried, but with a few key components. First, you visualize the other person standing in front of you; second, you dump and let them have it; and third, you say you're sorry and ask for forgiveness.

So the first step is to visualize the person or the person's "higher self" standing in front of you. It's very important to clarify that the person that you're having this conversation with is *not* in the room with you. You are by yourself. Under normal circumstances, yelling at people and telling them off doesn't improve relationships, but the imagined virtual being can handle it just fine. In actuality you might be speaking to a tree, or a chair, or a steering wheel in the car; but you visualize the person standing in front of you, and you imagine asking for their permission to talk to them.

The second step is to let them have it. Tell them all the things you've been holding back. You might even be yelling and swearing, and that's a good thing. Just get it all out. When you can't think of anything else to say, then it's time for the final step.

The third and final step is to apologize to this person for feeling all those negative thoughts and emotions towards them, and ask for forgiveness for anything you may have done that harmed them. Apologizing brings healing.

Some people have tried the virtual conversation and reported that it didn't create any closure or healing, but that's always because they left out that last crucial step of saying sorry and asking for forgiveness. "But it's not my fault, I didn't do anything wrong, it was all the other guy," they will say. Sometimes, that may be true, such as in the story of Corrie Ten Boom. She was an innocent victim, what could she possibly have to apologize for? She could express remorse for her negative feelings. Saying, "I'm sorry for my unkind feelings," is a way of acknowledging that you have those feelings, which is a necessary step in letting them go.

In our first discussion about journaling, we talked about how when we encode an event into our memory, our brain actually includes all the experiences that go with it, including all of our emotions that we felt at the time. When we recall a memory, it is a little like checking a book out from the library, and we also recall the emotions attached to those experiences which have been recorded in our body. But research indicates that when the memory is "checked out" of our long term memory, it becomes malleable, and we can make changes to it.[202]

At that point, we can soften or remove the negative emotions before we check the memory back into our brain, and it won't be as painful to recall the next time. However, we can also add additional negative emotions before we return that memory. This can happen when we ruminate and cycle our thoughts over and over, while adding more and more negative emotions to the event each time we think about it. This type of cycle is damaging, and is certainly not the objective of this exercise.

The process during a virtual conversation of allowing ourselves to feel our feelings, and get them out, is very cathartic and therapeutic; but, if we then re-attach all that energy before checking the memory back in, it will exacerbate the negative feelings. Adding an apology and asking for forgiveness in the third step of the virtual conversation is a necessary antidote to negate this potential problem.

Remember that the virtual conversation is done on your own, without the other person present. If, after the virtual conversation, you still feel that you need to have a discussion directly with the person, you will be better able to communicate without the interference of overwhelming emotions.

Here's an example of a virtual conversation. The event was that I was pruning our fruit trees, and although my husband was home and available, he left me to do all the work myself, again. That in and of itself was extremely frustrating, but what happened next made it worse. When I finished trimming the last branch, after hours of working alone, my husband walked up and took the pruning clippers from my hands. Then he trimmed a single branch. In fact, it was a branch that I had already trimmed; he just made it a few inches shorter, and then he walked away.

The final straw was when he told our grown daughter about his day, and he said, "Your mom and I pruned the fruit trees today," giving himself full credit as an equal partner. I was so angry I could have exploded, and I knew that I was feeling too emotional to say anything without lashing out, so I stayed silent.

To work out my frustration, I tried using the virtual conversation tool. It went something like this: First, I found a place where I could be alone and then visualized my husband standing in front of me. "Lewis, can I please speak to your higher self? I am so mad at you I could scream! How dare you tell Sarah that you pruned the trees when you did nothing but putter around your shop all day, and then take the pruners from my hand and snip one little branch! Did you really think that was helpful? How many times have you left me to do all the work alone?" And the rant continued until I couldn't think of anything else to say.

I paused to take a few cleansing breaths before continuing, "I know you weren't raised with an example of helping around the house or yard, and I know that our yard doesn't mean as much to you as it does to me. Next time I'll make sure to clearly and kindly ask for your help, because I really need you. I'm sorry for my unkind feelings towards you, will you forgive me?"

I paused for a moment while imagining him saying, "Of course I forgive you, will you forgive me too?"

"Yes, I forgive you."

Did it help? It certainly helped me. My overwhelming anger subsided and I could carry on. I didn't feel the need for a follow up discussion with Lewis after the virtual conversation. I realized that I could have done a better job in asking and making my needs known. Even though we didn't talk about it directly, an interesting thing happened the following year. It was time to prune the trees again, and Lewis immediately volunteered to help. We worked side by side pruning the trees, and the job took less than half as long. He offered before I even had a chance to ask. Did the virtual conversation have anything to do with it? I don't know, but it didn't hurt.

Day 23 - Connect with nature and/or exercise

Today's action step is to spend 30 minutes connecting with nature and/or exercising. If you need a reminder of what to do, or why to do it, please review the information for day 2.

Day 24 - Social support network diagram

The purpose of today's action step is to assess and increase your awareness of your social support network. Sometimes when we're feeling stressed and overwhelmed, we feel like we're carrying the whole world on our shoulders, and we're totally alone. However, even though we might feel like we're alone, that's often not really the case. There is a difference between our perception of social support and the actual support available.

There are different kinds of support that we might need.

<u>Emotional support</u> is someone with a listening ear, who will show compassion and empathy. They provide companionship and a sense of belonging. This might include friends, family members, significant others, co-workers, clergy members, or others. Some people include their pets in this category. Animals can provide wonderful emotional support.

<u>Informational support</u> is someone who can give good advice or help you work through your problems. Sometimes that's a friend or family member, but sometimes we turn to professionals like doctors, lawyers, or accountants for informational support. The internet is also a frequently used resource to search for answers.

<u>Practical support</u> is tangible or includes an action of some kind. If I don't have food, clothing, or I can't pay my rent, a listening ear is nice, but I also need practical support of some kind. I need food, clothes, money, or a solution of some kind. Practical support might include someone who's willing to tend your children, or drive you to a doctor's appointment, or help with food or rent. Sources of practical support might include family members, church, community, or government resources. Practical support is best used as a temporary scaffold to support you while you're building

something great inside, rather than a permanent crutch. Always work towards self-reliance, and then eventually you'll be in a position to pay it forward and help the next person who needs a helping hand.

Social support diagram

We're going to visually represent the resources in your support network with a diagram that looks something like a solar system, with your name in the center and a few concentric rings. We're going to write in the names of friends, family members, significant others, as well as other resources including church, community, and government resources on the diagram. Those people and resources that you feel close to you, will be listed within the inner circle. Those that you are a little less comfortable with, are placed in the outer circle. And those resources that exist, but you aren't likely to ask for help, can be outside the rings somewhere.

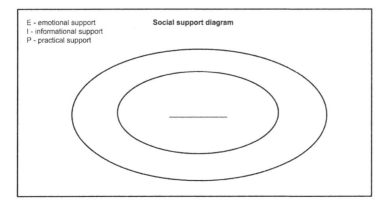

After listing these people and resources, I want you to think about what kind of support they might be able to provide. Can they help with emotional support, informational support, or practical support? On the chart place a letter E - emotional, I-informational, or P-practical next to each of the resources.

Here's an example from the granola days story in the introduction. Even though we felt totally alone, if we mapped out our resources, we actually had several people and places where we could go to get help. In the example, I kept things pretty general, but on your diagram you can be more specific by listing specific names of people, and specific things they can help with, like babysitting, etc.

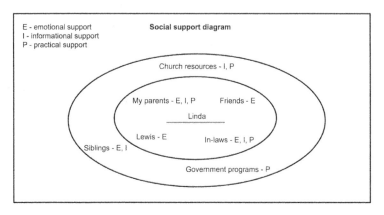

Day 25 - Finding solutions - part 1

The purpose for the action step today is to begin looking for answers to your problems. Remember that you are the expert on you and your situation. Chances are that you already have many of the answers already inside of you, but until you can calm down enough to get a greater perspective, you might not be able to see them. One way to see that you really do have solutions inside you, is to pretend that you're giving advice to someone else, and that's part of what we're going to do today.

We're going to fill out a chart that includes a stressful event or situation, our thoughts and emotions relating to that event (similar to the CBT triangle we did earlier), but we're also going to add two more things. One is where we look to see if there are any automatic thoughts and cognitive distortions like: personalization, selective attention/mental filtering, fortune telling, mind reading, catastrophizing, overgeneralization, labeling, shoulding and musting, emotional reasoning, magnification and minimization, black and white/all-or-nothing thinking (aka perfectionism). The final column is self-advice. If this were a friend coming to you for advice, what would you recommend?

Finding solutions - self recommendations

Event	Thoughts	Recommendations
Emotions	Cognitive distortions?	

I'll give examples from the three stories from the introduction. In the near miss story where Lewis was flying up the canyon, my first advice would be never to fly up a canyon. If you want to view the scenery of the mountains, first climb to altitude for the top of the canyon, and fly *down* the canyon. Another piece of advice is to remember your own inherent self-worth; your friend's opinion of you is not that important. You don't need to prove anything to him.

Finding solutions - self recommendations

Event	Thoughts	Recommendations
Lewis flying up the canyon	I want Ron to be impressed We're going to die	Never fly up a canyon. (fly down a canyon) Remember your own inherent self-worth, your friend's opinion of you is not that important. You don't need to prove anything to him.
Emotions	Cognitive distortions?	
Pride Fear, worry, stress, anxiety, terror, panic	Pride, personalization, mind reading, using social comparison to determine self-worth	

In the second story of the dreaded phone calls, my advice would be to carefully review all the cognitive distortions, and notice that most of them stem from a lack of self-worth. By gaining confidence in my own inherent self-worth, those other issues fade away into manageable tasks. Another piece of advice is to stop procrastinating. I could use the 5 second rule (where you count down from five to one and then act immediately), listed in the first aid section of this book, to help me have the courage to act. Another possibility is to write down on the calendar that I will make the phone calls on Sunday at 7:00 PM. Writing down a specific date and time can help our brains put that worry on hold for a while. That way, I wouldn't need to worry and fret on Tuesday, Wednesday, Thursday, Friday, and Saturday. It would give me several days without feeling guilty and stressed, rather than feeling constantly guilty and stressed. Then

I could use the 5 second rule and the virtual shield to help me get through the anxiety of making the calls on Sunday at 7:00 PM.

Finding solutions- self recommendations

Event	Thoughts	Recommendations
Dreaded phone calls	I don't want to do this, They're going to reject me, Nobody likes me, I don't know what to say	Remember your own inherent self-worth, Don't procrastinate
Emotions Fear, worry, stress, anxiety, dread, guilt	Cognitive distortions? personalization, mind reading, selective attention, catastrophizing, fortune telling, emotional reasoning, overgeneralization	Write date/time to call on calendar Use 5 second rule for confidence and action

In the granola days example, my advice would be to take a good look at the social resource diagram. With very little income, and the need for additional education and training, we needed immediate practical support. For us, the best solution was to allow our extended family into our circle of concern. We let them know about our dire financial situation, and asked for advice and help. We moved out of our apartment into my parents' basement to reduce expenses, so our limited income could be used for education and training to further Lewis' career. We had to get over some of our cognitive distortions, such as thinking our self-worth was tied to our finances and success, but it all worked out.

Finding solutions- self recommendations

Event	Thoughts	Recommendations
Granola days/poverty The landlady is raising the rent	How are we going to pay the rent? I'm embarrassed that we're so poor. We're worse off than a teenage mom on welfare. We're never going to be successful.	Remember your own inherent self-worth, Worth is not based on wealth.
Emotions	Cognitive distortions?	Social resources diagram - where can we turn for help?
Fear, worry, stress, anxiety, shame, panic, discouraged, depressed, hopeless	personalization, selective attention, catastrophizing, fortune telling, emotional reasoning, labeling, overgeneralization, etc.	Move into parents' basement - save money and work on furthering Lewis' training and education

Day - 26 Finding solutions - health related stress

During these last few days, we'll be looking closer at a few common stressors, starting with health related stress. Our physical health influences every aspect of our lives. Do you have any concerns about your health? Start with the basic questions: How bad is this? Can I survive this? Is it permanent? Is it temporary? Can I put it into perspective? If you're enjoying good or moderate health, perhaps health stress is just taking preventative measures or doing something to boost energy. If you're dealing with a chronic illness, then evaluating a social support diagram might be helpful, or working on finding meaning and purpose, or increasing the positive feelings of gratitude. You are the expert on your situation.

Today's action step is to fill out a chart like the one you did yesterday, and give yourself advice on any health related concerns you may have.

Day 27 - Connect with nature and/or exercise

Today's action step is to spend 30 minutes connecting with nature and/or exercising. If you need a reminder of what to do, or why to do it, please review the information for day 2.

Day 28 - Finding solutions - work related stress

Today we'll be looking for solutions to stressors related to work. Americans spend an average of 1800 hours at work per year, totaling about 90,000 hours of work during their lifetime.[203] Numerous studies show that job stress is by far the major source of stress for American adults, and that it has escalated progressively over the past few decades.[204]

According to reports done by the National Institute for Occupational Safety and Health (NIOSH)[205] and Attitudes in the American Workplace[206]

- 80% of workers feel stress on the job, nearly half say they need help in learning how to manage stress

- 40% of workers reported their job was very or extremely stressful

- 25% view their jobs as the number one stressor in their lives

- 75% of employees believe that workers have more on-the-job stress than a generation ago

- 26% of workers said they were often or very often burned out or stressed by their work

- Job stress is more strongly associated with health complaints than financial or family problems

In addition to all the tools we've been discussing on how to cope with general stress, such as exercise, somatic quieting, and becoming aware of cognitive distortions, here are a few suggestions to reduce stress at work.

Clarify expectations. One factor that contributes to job burnout is unclear requirements. If you don't know what is expected, or the requirements keep changing with little notice, it adds to the stress load. If this is a problem at work, it may help to be proactive and talk with your supervisor. Ask for clarification of expectations, and strategies for meeting them. This can relieve stress for both of you.

Stay Organized. Planning ahead and staying organized can greatly decrease stress at work. Being organized with your time means less rushing in the morning to avoid being late, and rushing to get out at the end of the day. Keeping yourself organized means avoiding the negative effects of clutter, and being more efficient with your work. One suggestion to improve organization is to write a simple to-do list of your top six priorities or tasks. By keeping it short, it seems doable, and prioritizing can help reduce the temptation to get sidetracked by less important things.

Get Comfortable. Do what you can to ensure that you're working from a quiet, comfortable, and soothing workspace. Physical discomfort can greatly add to your stress. If an uncomfortable chair causes a sore back, then it's time to invest in a new chair. Simple environmental changes in terms of light, temperature, noise, and space or privacy can make a big difference in your comfort level.

Chunk, don't multitask. Multitasking was once heralded as a fantastic way to maximize one's time and get more done in a day. However, research shows speed and accuracy suffer with multitasking. Multitasking also leads to a stressful kind of frazzled feeling. A new approach is called "chunking." Chunking is the concept of breaking up your day into larger chunks instead of reacting to constant interruptions. The more chunks of time you can devote to specific tasks, the fewer start-up moments you will have, and your efficiency improves dramatically.[207]

<u>Strive for excellence</u>. We discussed previously the difference between striving for excellence and its counterfeit known as perfectionism. Perfectionism can be a huge factor in creating stress at work. Please choose to let go of perfectionistic tendencies at work, and replace them with the healthier option of striving for excellence. Just do your best, and then congratulate yourself for your efforts and your successes. Your results will actually be better, and you'll be much less stressed at work.

<u>Walk at lunch</u>. We've discussed the importance and value of physical activity as a de-stressor. Taking a few moments to walk during a lunch break can help life mood, clear stress, and increase creativity and productivity when you return.

<u>Avoid interpersonal conflict</u>. The basic workload is enough stress without adding interpersonal conflict into the mix. Although that can be challenging, there are a few tips that may help. Be kind, respectful, and considerate of co-workers. Don't participate in gossip, and steer clear of hot topics like politics, lifestyle, or religious differences. Limit interactions with those co-workers who don't work well with others.

<u>Strengthen conflict resolution skills</u>. Sometimes, despite our best efforts, conflict finds us anyway. If that happens, it's time to pull out your conflict resolution skills. Stay calm and respectful. Don't become defensive. Avoid blaming and interrupting. Become aware of your own automatic thoughts, and look for cognitive distortions. Use neutral "I" statements rather than accusative "you" statements. For example, "I think...," "I'm not feeling understood...," or "I'm feeling disrespected by...," rather than "You always...," "You never...," or "You're such a ..." statements.

<u>Watch for cognitive distortions</u> including: personalization, selective attention/mental filtering, fortune telling, mind reading, catastrophizing, overgeneralization, labeling, shoulding and musting, emotional reasoning, magnification and minimization, black and white/all-or-nothing/perfectionism thinking. All of these distortions interfere with effective communication and conflict resolution.

<u>Focus on the present.</u> When we get frustrated with another person, it's tempting to bring up memories of past conflicts you've had with that person and add them to the current issue. This "kitchen sinking" approach escalates and encourages retaliation. It's like throwing gasoline on a fire, which is the opposite of conflict resolution. If someone uses this "kitchen sink" approach on you, rather than continuing the escalation, you might say, "Let's focus on the issue at hand."

<u>Use active listening.</u> Sometimes, we're so concerned about being heard, we forget to listen. You don't have to agree with that person, but you can try to understand where they're coming from. Oftentimes, when a person feels like you're listening, they are more likely to listen to you as well. Even though you may not be able to solve your personal issues with the other person, you can definitely work on the tangible issues that interfere with cooperation in meeting goals.

<u>Pay attention to non-verbal communication.</u> Body language can tell you when someone is saying one thing but means another. By being emotionally aware, you can notice when someone's posture, gestures, or facial expressions differ from their words. When someone says, "I'm fine," you can tell they're not fine if they avert their eyes. Then, you can create an environment that makes that person feel more comfortable being honest with you.

<u>Take a vacation</u>. According to a study released by the U.S. Travel Association, 55 percent of Americans did not use all their paid vacation time. In 2018, Americans left 768 million days of paid time off unused.[208] Taking a break from work can be like pressing a reset button. It can help people be more productive when they return to business.

What else?

If you've done everything and you still are stressed by a toxic job or a toxic boss, then step back and take a critical look at whether or not you need to find the courage to end a job, and move on somewhere else. We have a friend who felt overwhelmed by his stressful job and the pressures he felt in his keep-up-with-the-Jones's neighborhood, so he quit his job, moved across the country, and fulfilled his personal dream of owning a used book store. Money isn't everything. You're allowed to prioritize happiness.

Day 29 - Core beliefs about money

Financial matters often are a source of fear, anxiety, worry, and stress. Today's action step is to increase your awareness about your core beliefs about money.

We've already investigated how hidden core beliefs about worry and forgiveness may keep us from letting go of some of our burdens, in a similar fashion our unconscious core beliefs about money may contribute to some of our worries and frustrations about money and wealth. Your core beliefs about money might be called your "money script." Money scripts are the unconscious beliefs about money that are often learned in childhood, and passed down from generation to generation. Research shows that our unconscious money scripts have been found to be associated with our income, net worth, credit card and other debt, financial outcomes, financial behaviors, and other aspects of financial health.[209] We'll review four basic core money beliefs: money avoidance, money worship, money status, and money vigilance. We may carry beliefs from more than one category, even when the categories seem to contradict each other.

Money avoidance

Money avoiders believe it's selfish to want a lot of money. They believe that money is the root of all evil. They tend to view money as negative and a source of fear, anxiety, or disgust. Money avoidance can be associated with trying to not think about money, ignoring financial statements, overspending, enabling others financially, or having difficulty managing a budget. They may believe that wealthy people are greedy or corrupt, and that there is virtue in being poor, or having just enough to meet your needs. Money avoiders often think that they don't deserve money. Because of their negative associations with money and people who are wealthy, they may unconsciously sabotage their financial success.[210] Many money avoiders are just trying to be good people, and they assume that they have to be poor in order to be good. Here's an alternate suggestion. Instead of thinking money is evil, try this thought, "The money I earned is evidence of the value I created for others."

Money worship

Money worshipers, on the other hand, believe that the key to happiness, and the solution to their problems is to have more money. They think, "All my problems would be solved if I just had enough money," or, "I would be happy if I were rich." For these people money is viewed as a scarce resource, and there will never be enough of it. Money worshipers are prone to buying things in an attempt to achieve happiness, and often have a lot of credit card debt. Because they believe that money and wealth are what bring happiness and satisfaction, they may prioritize work over family and social relationships.[211]

Money status

Money status seekers tend to define their self-worth by their financial net worth. They may pretend to possess more wealth than they actually have, and may overspend to provide others with an impression they have achieved financial success. They tend to spend lavishly on outward displays of wealth by buying the hottest new items or name brands, and as a result can be at risk of overspending. Excessive money status seekers are more likely to overspend, gamble excessively, be financially dependent on others, and hide expenditures from their spouses.[212]

Money vigilance

Money vigilance is typically associated with frugality. People with these money beliefs tend to focus on the importance of saving, use discretion when discussing financial matters, and express anxiety about not saving enough for emergencies. Money vigilant people are most likely to pay attention to their financial well-being. They are less likely to buy on credit, and have higher levels of financial health. A common belief for the money vigilant is that people should work hard for their money and not expect financial handouts. They also tend to be more anxious and guarded when discussing money matters with people outside of their closest network of friends and family. While money vigilance encourages saving and frugality, when carried to extremes, it can also lead to excessive wariness or anxiety that can prevent them from enjoying the benefits, and sense of security that money can provide.[213]

Journaling to increase awareness of core beliefs about money. Spend 20-30 minutes writing about one of more of the following prompts:

- What are your current "money scripts" or financial belief patterns?

- Where did those core beliefs about money come from?

- Do your money beliefs support your life goals or are they creating a roadblock?

Day 30 - Finding solutions - money related stress

Today's action step is to begin looking for solutions to any stressors relating to money. Becoming aware is the first step to empower yourself to make any necessary changes. Hopefully the journaling exercise from yesterday helped you become aware of your core beliefs about money. Remember from the CBT triangle that our thoughts, our emotions, and our behaviors/actions are highly interconnected. Improving financial health requires changes in behavior, but those changes aren't likely to take place if they're not in line with your emotions and thoughts regarding money.

Money scripts are unconscious beliefs about money, and they usually are formed in childhood. As an adult, you have the opportunity to change those beliefs, and create new patterns. In actuality, money is neither good nor bad; it is neutral. What makes it "good" or "bad" is our attitude towards it, how we earned it, and/or how we choose to spend it.

Here are a few proven strategies to improve your financial well-being which helps alleviate fear, anxiety, worry and stress about money.[214, 215, 216]

Avoid debt

If you're looking for ways to reduce fear, anxiety, worry and stress about money, then the number one financial priority is getting out of debt and staying out of debt. Debt is spending your future income. Then when the paycheck comes, it's already spent, and that can be really discouraging. And if, for some reason, you don't get a paycheck, then worry and anxiety can skyrocket. Research shows that the stress from debt can lead to health problems including ulcers, migraines, depression, and even heart attacks. The deeper you get into debt, the more likely it is that you will face health complications.[217]

Debt can also seriously harm your relationships. In a study of more than 4500 married couples, researchers saw that couples who took on more debt over time became more likely to split up. Couples with higher debt also fought more about money, and reported lower marital satisfaction. In fact, in general, fighting over money is a major cause of divorce.[218]

Debt encourages you to spend more than you can afford. Part of the allure of debt is the fact that you can get the emotional high from getting what you want now, whether or not you have the money to pay for it. But eventually, that spending will catch up with you, with interest! Because of the accrued interest, debt makes everything more expensive. You end up paying more, sometimes much more, than the original price of the item. For example, let's say you used your credit card to buy new furniture for your living room. The price of the furniture was $2,000. You make the minimum payments each month, and your credit card has a low interest rate of 11%. It seems like a pretty good deal until you do the math. By the time the furniture is paid off, you actually spent $3,600 for the furniture. That's an additional $1,600!

Furthermore, monthly debt payments limit the amount of money you have to spend on other things. The more debt you accumulate, the higher your monthly payments will be, and the less you have to spend on everything else.

Saving

After debts are paid off, the next step to financial security is saving for an emergency fund. Life has a tendency to throw us curves. Things come up that we weren't expecting like a job loss, or the car needs new tires, or someone needs to go to the hospital, or whatever. These things happen; they're a part of life. If you have some savings on hand, then these unexpected things won't be so stressful. Being prepared can reduce a lot of worry and anxiety.

Being prepared is also very important when it comes to aging. Those who prepare for retirement by saving and investing look forward to it, while those who don't prepare begin to panic when they near retirement age. Preparation is easier and more effective when you begin to plan, save, and invest early in adulthood and continue throughout your working lifetime.

Finding solutions - money related stress

Today's action step is to begin looking for solutions to any stressors relating to money. In a nutshell, being financially stable is about spending less than you earn. There are two ways to approach this. One is to increase income, and the other is to decrease expenses. And of course, you can do both.

If worrying about money is affecting your life, look for ways to reduce expenses. For example, you might cancel your cable or satellite TV subscription, or pack a lunch rather than going out to eat every day. Run the numbers and see how much you can save. You are the expert on your situation. You know your income; you know your expenses (or if you don't, you can do some research and figure it out).

Today's assignment is to fill out a chart including your thoughts, emotions, and behaviors about money. Also fill out any money scripts that you may notice. In the final column, give yourself some recommendations to improve your financial health, which will in turn reduce your fears, anxieties, worries, and stresses about money related matters. You got this!

7.

BUILDING ON MAGNIFICENT
MOMENTUM

Building on magnificent momentum

You are now empowered with a full set of tools to calm fear, anxiety, worry and stress so that you can experience more joy, satisfaction, and peace in your life. You may find that you need more than 30 days to complete the exercises in this book, and that's perfectly okay. You may want to spend several days, or maybe even weeks or months, practicing and building particular skills that will be most beneficial to you. You may need to take longer breaks before delving into a new technique, and that's okay too.

However you choose to implement these tools, I hope that you will keep going, and continue to build on the magnificent momentum you've gained.

To stay mentally and emotionally strong and resilient, I recommend maintaining the habits of a morning routine, daily action step, and an evening routine. You can use this book as a template, or create your own. You have the tools; you have the power.

You got this!

Appendix A

Emotional First Aid Kit

Emotional first aid kit

The following section is a list of tools to use as an emotional first aid kit. Remember that an emotional first aid kit is just a list of tools that can provide an immediate, although temporary, positive effect. Use these anytime you hit an emotional wall, feel overwhelmed, or you just need a quick boost. Stick with me. You got this. You can knock those walls over, and turn them into stairs that will take you to a higher, happier plane.

Sing a song 3X

If you find yourself in a rough spot, sing along to an upbeat, positive song. Sing through one song three times, or sing three different positive upbeat songs once. Print out the lyrics so you can sing all the words, and choose songs that have lyrics that have meaning to you personally. Here are a few suggested songs to help you create your own list: *Roar* by Katy Perry, *Try Everything* by Shakira, *Waka Waka* by Shakira, *Brave* by Sara Bareilles, *Unwritten* by Natasha Bedingfield, *Fight Song* by Rachel Platten, *Happy* by Pharrel Williams, *Better When I'm Dancin'* by Meghan Trainor, *On Top of the World* by Imagine Dragons, *Believer* by Imagine Dragons, and *You Are Loved* by Stars Go Dim.

5 second rule

The 5 second rule is simple; it's like a countdown for a launch. If there's something you know you should do, but need a boost to actually do it, start counting down from 5 like this 5, 4, 3, 2, 1, and then do it immediately. The idea behind the 5 second rule is simple: if you have an impulse to act on a goal, you must physically move within 5 seconds or fear may set in, and you'll talk yourself out of it.

Boost confidence and mood with a power pose

You can improve your mood in just 90 seconds by doing this one simple trick. Put your chin up, smile (even if you don't feel like it). Pull your shoulders back; stand straight and tall with your hands relaxed at your sides, or on your hips. Keep both feet pointing forward, and keep weight even on both legs. Hold this position for 90 seconds.

Connect with nature

Spending time outside in nature is good for the body and the mind. It helps distract us from problems, and just helps us feel good. If the weather permits, take off your shoes and feel the grass or sand under your feet. Feel the warmth of the sun, and the coolness of the breeze, and feel your body moving as you walk. Hear the birds, or the waves, or the rustle of the grass in the wind. Smell the flowers and the trees, and see the beauty of nature around you. Enjoy a sensory experience in nature and feel its calming effects.

Take a walk

Virtually any form of exercise can act as a stress reliever. Exercise does wonderful things to help our emotional well-being. It increases the production of endorphins, which are the brain's feel-good neurotransmitters. Walking, jogging, and other forms of exercise that use large muscle groups in a repetitive motion are also forms of moving meditation. These moving meditations provide similar benefits to traditional meditation by calming us down, and distracting us from our problems. It improves mood, helps us relax and improves quality of sleep. So if you're feeling stressed out, it might be a good idea to pause and go for a walk

Visualize a shield

If you're struggling with feelings of fear and vulnerability, visualizing a shield can be a way to help you feel safer. Creating a shield basically means imagining, visualizing, intending, and feeling that you are completely surrounded by a force field or shield. Be creative and specific in imagining what it looks like, what color it is, how it feels inside and any other specific details you can think of. Imagine that negative comments are deflected by the shield. They don't even reach you, and they can't get inside you. You allow them to bounce off into space where they are harmless. Choose to allow positive comments to flow through the shield. The shield is a filter, not a wall.

2-minute distraction

If you can succeed in changing your mental channel for at least two minutes, you have a chance of breaking that destructive cycle of rumination. Take action to break free of them and attain a fresh perspective. Become immersed in a great book that moves you, or watch a movie that transports you. Exercise. Go for a walk. In short, do what you know from experience bounces your thinking to a more optimistic place.

Laughter

When looking for an excellent distraction, laughter really is the best medicine. Laughter stops distressing emotions. It helps you shift perspective, allowing you to see situations in a more realistic, less threatening light. So what makes you laugh? A good joke? Funny cat videos? Make a list of things that make you laugh and keep them on hand, because nothing works faster, or more dependably, to bring your mind and body back into balance than a good laugh.

Mini-meditation

There are many studies that verify that meditation eases anxiety and mental stress. Here's a mini meditation exercise that you can do anytime, anywhere, to help calm you down in just a few seconds. With your hands in front of you, line up the tips of the fingers of your left hand to the corresponding tips of the fingers of your right hand. Take 5 slow, deep belly breaths while pressing the fingertips against each other with medium force. Shake out your hands, and relax them to your sides or your lap, and take one last slow, deep breath.

Connect with friends

Make a list of the people you can turn to. These are people that you trust to support you, and make an effort to contact them regularly. Reach out to them, and ask for specific kinds of help. Remember, your friends can't read your mind, and it's not fair to expect them to.

Replace rumination with positive affirmations

If a thought keeps running through your mind like, "I'm not good enough," replace it with another opposite and positive statement such as, "I am worthy and deserving of being loved, valued and appreciated. I am loved, valued and appreciated. I am good enough." And repeat that over and over again. There's a lot of truth taught in the children's book "The Little Engine That Could" by Watty Piper. Repeating, "I think I can, I think I can," or whatever positive mantra is applicable, really makes a difference.

Pet the dog

If you're feeling anxious, stressed, depressed or lonely, one thing that might help is to spend some time petting a dog or cat. Research shows that playing with, or petting an animal can reduce stress, and can also help us reduce feelings of isolation, and help us feel more connected. Petting a dog or cat increases oxytocin production in the brain, which lowers stress and increases feelings of happiness. It also decreases production of cortisol, which is a stress hormone, so it works in multiple ways to help you calm down and feel better.

Small act of service

Anxiety, worry, and fear tend to make a person retreat inward. Helping other people can help bring us outside ourselves. It can also help distract us from our own problems, and think about something else. Studies have shown that people who help others have lowered levels of depression and anxiety. In fact, in the research study, service was more effective in making a positive difference in the way participants felt about themselves, than making an effort to pamper themselves, or creating self-esteem goals.

APPENDIX B

COGNITIVE DISTORTIONS

Cognitive distortions

Automatic thoughts are often done out of habit, and we don't even realize that we're doing it. Unfortunately, these automatic thoughts usually include assumptions or patterns often called "cognitive distortions," because they don't accurately reflect what's going on. The following is a list of cognitive distortions, as well as questions we might ask ourselves, in order to give a more balanced and accurate perspective:

Personalization is the tendency to take everything very personally. This can either come in the form of assuming that something was intended as a personal attack, or it might manifest in a belief that everything that happened is all our fault. We're personally to blame for everything. Balancing question - Is there another way of looking at this? Who or what else may have played a part in this?

Selective attention/mental filtering is the tendency to focus on negative events, while filtering out or ignoring the positive events, or things that went well. Balancing question - What are the positives in this situation? Did anything go right?

Fortune telling is a form of jumping to conclusions, where we assume we know what will happen in the future. Usually fortune telling includes pessimistic thinking or what could go wrong. Balancing question - What evidence do I have to support this conclusion? Is there another possible outcome?

Mind reading is another form of jumping to conclusions, where we assume that we know what someone else is thinking. These conclusions are rarely, if ever, based on facts or concrete evidence, but rather based on personal feelings and opinions. As a result, they can often lead us astray. Balancing question - What evidence do I have to support this conclusion? Is there any evidence that supports a different conclusion? Can I clarify with this person what they're actually thinking?

Catastrophizing is the tendency to blow circumstances out of proportion, and make things out to be a lot worse than they should be; basically we're making mountains out of molehills. It's helpful to gain perspective by asking yourself a few questions: How bad is this? Can I survive this? Is it permanent? Is it temporary? Balancing question - Is it possible that things aren't as bad as I make them out to be?

Overgeneralization is when we tend to make broad generalizations that are based on a single event, and minimal evidence. A clue that we might be using overgeneralization, is when we use phrases that include the words *never* or *always*. For example, "You always..." or "He never..." In these instances, we are using a past event to predict all future events. Balancing question - Can I think of any instances where that was not the case? Is any evidence suggesting that things could now be different?

Labeling is the tendency to make global statements about ourselves, or others, based on behavior in a specific situation. For example, "I'm a failure!" or "You are an insensitive jerk." It changes a specific behavior or incident, and turns it into an all-encompassing definition. I/you/he /she/they = _____. Balancing question - Is there evidence that this is true in all situations? Can I think of any evidence that is contrary to this conclusion?

Shoulding and musting is the tendency to make unrealistic and unreasonable demands on yourself and others. "I should have done this," or, "She should have done that." This is unhelpful because it sets people up for failure, and also doesn't take into account other alternatives. Balancing question - Is there another way to do things that I haven't yet considered? Might there be more than one way to do things?

Emotional reasoning is a cognitive distortion where we tend to interpret our experience of reality, based upon how we are feeling in the moment. Our emotional state skews our interpretation of the actual event. Balancing question - Is there any evidence that how I'm seeing this isn't accurate? Is it possible that my emotions affected my interpretation of what really happened?

Magnification and minimization is a cognitive distortion where we tend to magnify the positive attributes of another person, while minimizing our own positive attributes. We often compare someone else's highlight reel with our blooper reel. This devalues ourselves while putting someone else on a pedestal. Balancing question - What talents and abilities do I have? Find evidence that you, too, are deserving and capable.

Black and white/All-or-nothing thinking/Perfectionism refers to thinking in extremes. You are either a success or a failure. Your performance was totally good or totally bad. If you are not perfect, then you are a failure. This binary way of thinking leads to unreasonable expectations, and low self-esteem, and/or harsh criticism of others. Balancing question - What are the positives in this situation? Did anything go right? Is it possible that rather than being entirely black or white, it was actually a shade of gray?

Appendix C

Instructions for Morning Routine

Morning routine (complete before noon) - this should take about 15 minutes

Do one simple thing to nourish and support your body (choose one)

- Good quality vitamin supplement with B-complex vitamins or

- Green smoothie or

- Wheatgrass

Empowering (do both)

- "I am" poster (two minutes) while listening to music and

- Positive affirmations (three times) while listening to music

Building feelings of peace and safety (choose one)

- Creating a virtual shield or

- Loving-kindness meditation

"I am" poster

Spend two minutes looking at, and pondering the "I am" poster with
instrumental (epic) background music.

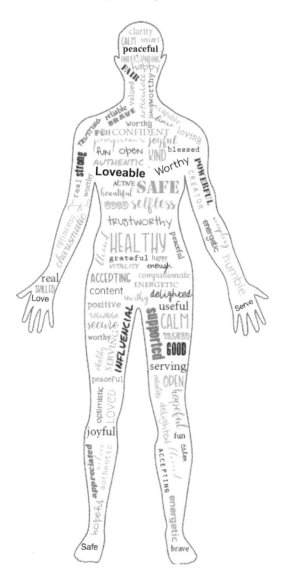

Positive affirmations

Repeat three times with instrumental (epic) background music

- I am at peace with myself, with others, and with my life circumstances.

- I willingly let go of any unnecessary fear, anxiety, worry, and stress.

- I allow peace, and feelings of safety, to flow into my heart and my mind, and I experience joy and delight each day.

- I am creative, capable, and confident.

- I open my eyes, my mind, and my heart to find solutions to my problems, and I'm delighted that it is easier than I ever thought possible.

Creating a virtual shield

Creating a shield basically means imagining, visualizing, intending, and feeling that you are completely surrounded by a force field or shield. Mental creation with intention is a powerful thing. Be creative and specific in imagining what it looks like, what color it is, how it feels inside, what temperature it is, and what it smells like. Notice the quality of the light and any other specific details you can think of. Imagine that negative comments are deflected by the shield. They don't even reach you, and they can't get inside you. You allow them to bounce off into space where they are harmless. Choose to allow positive comments to flow through the shield. The shield is a filter, not a wall.

Loving-kindness meditation

To begin, sit upright in a comfortable chair with both feet flat on the floor. Sit up straight and tall, not stiff, but upright. The reason we keep both feet on the floor is that we don't want crossing our legs to cause any blood flow restrictions. We want our blood and our energy to flow freely throughout the body, and we sit up tall for a similar reason. We don't want slouching to restrict our oxygen intake at all. We want to be able to breathe fully and deeply. As we breathe deeply, it enriches our blood with oxygen, which helps feed the cells in our bodies. Place one hand over your chest, and the other over your belly. Take a few deep breaths through your nose. Breathing through your nose naturally slows the breathing rate, since the nostrils are smaller openings than your mouth. Notice which hand is moving more. Practice until the hand over your belly is moving, and the hand over your chest is relatively still.

When you have the hang of it, you may rest your hands gently in your lap. Close your eyes to minimize distractions. Take a few deep breaths, and just relax and focus on the gentle sensation of breathing in and out.

Now I want you to pick an image of a person, just a mental image of someone you care about. It can be whoever you like, and just imagine you're looking at that person. While you're focusing on that image, we're going to say a simple mantra, and I want you to imagine that you're saying it to that person.

"May you be free. May you find peace. May you have grace and courage. May you be free. May you find peace. May you have grace and courage. May you be free. May you find peace. May you have grace and courage. May you be free. May you find peace. May you have grace and courage. May you be free. May you find peace. May you have grace and courage."

Now I'd like you to change the image, and I want you to imagine you're looking in a mirror. So you're looking at yourself as you repeat this mantra. This is a message for you.

"May you be free. May you find peace. May you have grace and courage. May you be free. May you find peace. May you have grace and courage. May you be free. May you find peace. May you have grace and courage. May you be free. May you find peace. May you have grace and courage. May you be free. May you find peace. May you have grace and courage."

Bring your attention back to your breath. Take a few more deep breaths, then gently open your eyes.

YOU GOT THIS!

Appendix D

INSTRUCTIONS FOR EVENING ROUTINE

Evening routine (complete before midnight) - about 15 minutes

Empowering (do both)

- "I am" poster (two minutes) while listening to music **and**

- Positive affirmations (three times) while listening to music

Somatic quieting through progressive relaxation

"I am" poster

Spend two minutes looking at, and pondering the "I am" poster with instrumental (epic) background music.

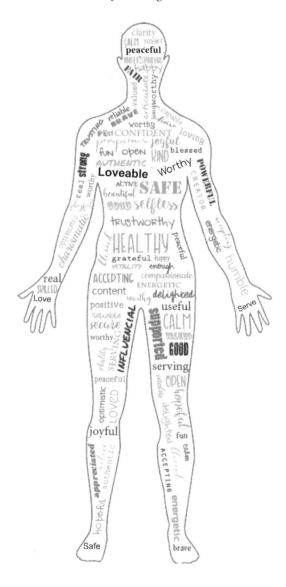

Positive affirmations

Repeat three times with instrumental (epic) background music

- I am at peace with myself, with others, and with my life circumstances.

- I willingly let go of any unnecessary fear, anxiety, worry, and stress.

- I allow peace, and feelings of safety to flow into my heart, and my mind, and I experience joy and delight each day.

- I am creative, capable, and confident.

- I open my eyes, my mind, and my heart to find solutions to my problems, and I'm delighted that it is easier than I ever thought possible.

Progressive muscle relaxation exercise

Lie down and get comfortable. First, you're going to focus on your breath. We're going to work on breathing slower and deeper. Take a few deep breaths through your nose. Breathing through your nose naturally slows the rate of breathing, because nostrils are smaller openings than your mouth, and it takes a little longer to inhale and exhale completely. Place one hand on your chest and one hand on your belly. Notice which hand is moving. When we are doing shallow chest breathing, the hand over your chest will move up and down; you also might notice your shoulders moving up and down. But if you're doing deep diaphragmatic breathing, then the hand over your belly will move, and the hand over your chest will hardly move at all as you breathe in and out. Practice a few times, feeling that hand over your belly moving up and down. When you feel comfortable that you're doing it well, then you can relax your hands into your lap, or at your sides.

Now, I'd like you to close your eyes to minimize distractions. We're going to give your eyes a rest and use some of your other senses right now.

Let yourself relax. Now I'm going to ask you to direct your attention to your toes and your feet. Now I'm going to ask you to scrunch up and tighten your toes. Squeeze the muscles in your toes, and feel the tightness. Feel a little bit of that tension in your toes, and hold it, hold it. Hold that tension and that tightness in your toes. And then just relax that tension. Relax your toes. Now imagine a warm wave of relaxation is washing over your toes. This wave of peace and relaxation is lapping at your feet, relaxing your feet and your toes.

Next we're going to move up to your calves. Tighten your calves by flexing your feet, bringing your toes up towards your body. Feel that large muscle getting a bit warmer as it is squeezing. Keep it tight, tight, tight. Feel the tension in your calves, feel that burn as you hold it tight. Then relax. Lower your toes back down, and shake your feet a little. Shake off that tension. Relax your calves and feel the nourishing blood rushing back to the muscles. Relax. Feel that wave of relaxation washing over your feet and your calves.

Next I'm going to ask you to tighten the muscles in your thighs and your backside. Squeeze your legs, and squeeze your bum cheeks together. Tighten all of those muscles and feel the tension. These are the largest muscles in the body. They are powerful. Squeeze and tighten them and hold them tight. Hold it, hold it, and now release all that tension. Allow all of that tightness and tension to leave your body. Notice the feel of the bed beneath you. Right now something else is supporting you, and those muscles in your body can have a rest. And because of that rest, they will be better able to serve you, and support you when you need them again. Right now they just get to relax. Feel that warm wave of relaxation now washing from your toes all the way up to your waist. Feel how these waves nourish your muscles and your body. As each wave recedes, it pulls out more tension and washes it away, and you feel your legs and lower half of your body completely relaxed.

Now we move up to the torso. Tighten your abdominal muscles like you're doing a sit up, or a crunch. Tighten and hold these muscles, feeling the tension in your stomach and lower back. Feel the squeeze, feel the tightness and just hold it. Hold it, hold the tension, and now release and relax the torso. Let it all go. Allow all of that tension to release and feel a wave of relaxation washing from your toes all the way up to your armpits. It's nourishing; it's relaxing. And as it recedes it pulls out any tension, any tightness, and any toxins that it finds and it washes them away.

Next we're going to go to your hands and your arms. I want you to make a tight fist. Make a really tight fist. You can feel it in your forearms; you can feel it in your hands. You can feel all the tightness and the tension in your hands and arms.

Just feel that squeeze and hold it. Now relax. Open your fist and allow the fingers to wiggle releasing any tension. Allow your hands to drop back to your sides. Let your fingers relax, let your arms relax. Imagine now that wave of relaxation is washing over your arms, your torso, and your legs. Allow the wave's nourishing and healing power to wash over you, and then notice how as it recedes it pulls out any remaining tension.

We'll go up to your shoulders, and I want you to raise your shoulders up to your ears. As you tighten these muscles, you feel it in your shoulders; you feel it across your upper back, and you feel it in your neck. Feel the tension, feel the tightness, and hold it. And then release it. Let your shoulders relax. Let your upper back relax. Let your neck relax. Imagine that wave of relaxation again washing from your toes to your neck, feeling it nourishing and relaxing as it washes over you, and pulling out any tension or toxins. This gentle wave is massaging away any tension leaving the muscles completely relaxed.

Now I want you to tense your face by pressing your lips together and scrunching your nose. Just press it together. Feel the tension, feel the tightness in those facial muscles; hold it, and then relax. Imagine now that you're in a deep warm bath completely covered and completely relaxed. As the gentle warmth enfolds you, it nourishes and heals your body and your mind, and washes away any tension.

Direct your attention back to your breath. Take a few nice deep, belly breaths, breathing through your nose. Now do a quick scan of your body starting with your toes, and working all the way up to the crown of your head. If there are any remaining spots of tension, imagine another gentle wave of relaxation is coming. This wave is massaging away any tension, and bringing a sense of calm and peace from your head to your toes.

Just continue to relax and breathe deeply, but we're going to help take your mind somewhere - somewhere that brings you peace or brings your joy. I want you to imagine your picture of paradise, a place where you would like to go. Maybe it's on a beach, or in a beautiful meadow, or a cabin in a forest. Wherever brings you peace and happiness.

I want you to look around this place that you're created. This is a place where you are absolutely safe. This is a place that is completely under your control. I want you to notice what's there. I want you to notice if there are other people around, or if you're there by yourself. Notice the light. Is it bright, or is it dim? Notice the temperature. Is it warm or is it cool? Notice any smells that are there. Do you smell flowers, pine trees, freshly baked chocolate chip cookies, or something else? Pay attention to any sounds that you might be hearing. Are there birds? Is there music? Allow yourself to enjoy a full sensory experience. This is a place that belongs to you. It is your space; you control it, and you can go back to this place any time that you want. It only takes a moment. Allow this place to feed you, to nourish your soul, to take away any stress or pain.

Take a few deep breaths. I want you to take one last look around your personal paradise, and remind yourself that you can come back here any time that you want. You're going to say goodbye for now, but you're going to make a promise to come back sometime soon. Again notice the sights, the sounds, the smells, and make that promise to come back.

Draw your attention back to your breath. Take a few deep, belly breaths, and come back to where you are. Open your eyes, wiggle your fingers and your toes. Your body and your mind are completely relaxed.

Appendix E

DAILY CHARTS AND INSTRUCTION

Day 1 – Journaling to reduce fear, anxiety, worry, and stress	Completed
Morning routine – complete before noon	
Nourishing and supporting your body • Vitamin supplement with B-complex vitamins **or** • Green smoothie **or** • Wheatgrass	
Empowering • "I am" poster (two minutes) with music **and** • Positive affirmations (three times) with music	
Building feelings of peace and safety • Create a virtual shield **or** • Loving-kindness meditation	
Daily action step – complete any time during the day	
Spend 20-30 minutes writing about one or more of the following prompts: • I feel fearful because… • I feel anxious because… • I feel worried because… • I feel stressed because...	
Evening routine – complete before midnight	
Empowering • "I am" poster (two minutes) with music **and** • Positive affirmations (three times) with music	
Somatic quieting • Progressive relaxation	

Day 1 – Journaling to reduce fear, anxiety, worry, and stress

Spend 20-30 minutes writing about one or more of the following prompts:

- I feel fearful because…

- I feel anxious because…

- I feel worried because…

- I feel stressed because...

_____

_____

_____

_____

_____

_____

_____

_____

_____

_____

_____

_____

_____

_____

_____

_____

_____

_____

_____

Somatic quieting

Because this journaling exercise may bring up negative emotions, which in turn may activate the body's stress response, we're going to do some somatic quieting afterwards to calm the body and the mind. You may choose from a couple of different options. You may try a mini-meditation, repeat either the virtual shield or loving-kindness meditation from the morning routine, or even something else that you know from experience helps you turn on that relaxation response.

How to do a mini-meditation

With your hands in front of you, line up the tips of the fingers of your left hand to the corresponding tips of the fingers of your right hand. Take five or more slow, deep belly breaths while pressing the fingertips against each other with medium force. Feel the pressure of the fingertips pressing together. Then shake out your hands, and relax them to your sides or your lap, and take a few more slow, deep breaths.

Day 2 – Connect with nature and/or exercise	Completed
Morning routine – complete before noon	
Nourishing and supporting your body • Vitamin supplement with B-complex vitamins **or** • Green smoothie **or** • Wheatgrass	
Empowering • "I am" poster (two minutes) with music **and** • Positive affirmations (three times) with music	
Building feelings of peace and safety • Create a virtual shield **or** • Loving-kindness meditation	
Daily action step – complete any time during the day	
Connect with nature and/or exercise (20-30 minutes)	
Evening routine – complete before midnight	
Empowering • "I am" poster (two minutes) with music **and** • Positive affirmations (three times) with music	
Somatic quieting • Progressive relaxation	

Day 2 – Connect with nature and/or exercise

Dedicate 20-30 minutes to calm the body and mind either by exercising, or by connecting with nature, and preferably by combining the two.

Virtually any form of exercise can act as a stress reliever, but activities such as walking or jogging that involve repetitive movements of large muscle groups can be particularly stress relieving, since they offer many of the same benefits as meditation.

Spending time in nature is good for the body and the mind. It helps relieve feelings of worry, anxiety and stress, and contributes to your physical wellbeing by reducing blood rate, heart rate, muscle tension, and the production of stress hormones.

This activity will obviously vary depending on season, location, or current weather conditions. If you can't go outside and take a walk, then just adapt, and do the best you can. Be creative. What can you do to create an interaction with nature?

• 	Take a walk through some beautiful natural scenery whether that be in a park, along a beach, a river trail, a mountain path, or just around the neighborhood.

• 	Mall-walk or use a treadmill while listening to a recording of nature sounds.

• 	Groom a desktop Zen garden or executive sandbox.

• 	Enjoy 30 minutes petting, playing with, and interacting with your pet.

Day 3 – Journaling to reduce fear, anxiety, worry, and stress	Completed
Morning routine – complete before noon	
Nourishing and supporting your body • Vitamin supplement with B-complex vitamins **or** • Green smoothie **or** • Wheatgrass	
Empowering • "I am" poster (two minutes) with music **and** • Positive affirmations (three times) with music	
Building feelings of peace and safety • Create a virtual shield **or** • Loving-kindness meditation	
Daily action step – complete any time during the day	
Spend 20-30 minutes writing about one or more of the following prompts: • I feel fearful because… • I feel anxious because… • I feel worried because… • I feel stressed because...	
Evening routine – complete before midnight	
Empowering • "I am" poster (two minutes) with music **and** • Positive affirmations (three times) with music	
Somatic quieting • Progressive relaxation	

Day 3 – Journaling to reduce fear, anxiety, worry, and stress

Spend 20-30 minutes writing about one or more of the following prompts:

- I feel fearful because…
- I feel anxious because…
- I feel worried because…
- I feel stressed because...

_____

_____

_____

_____

_____

_____

_____

_____

_____

_____

_____

_____

_____

_____

_____

_____

_____

_____

_____

YOU GOT THIS!

Somatic quieting

Because this journaling exercise may bring up negative emotions, which in turn may activate the body's stress response, we're going to do some somatic quieting afterwards to calm the body and the mind. You may choose from a couple of different options. You may try a mini-meditation, repeat either the virtual shield or loving-kindness meditation from the morning routine, or even something else that you know from experience helps you turn on that relaxation response.

How to do a mini-meditation

With your hands in front of you, line up the tips of the fingers of your left hand to the corresponding tips of the fingers of your right hand. Take five or more slow, deep belly breaths while pressing the fingertips against each other with medium force. Feel the pressure of the fingertips pressing together. Then shake out your hands, and relax them to your sides or your lap, and take a few more slow, deep breaths.

Day 4 – CBT triangle	Completed
Morning routine – complete before noon	
Nourishing and supporting your body • Vitamin supplement with B-complex vitamins **or** • Green smoothie **or** • Wheatgrass	
Empowering • "I am" poster (two minutes) with music **and** • Positive affirmations (three times) with music	
Building feelings of peace and safety • Create a virtual shield **or** • Loving-kindness meditation	
Daily action step – complete any time during the day	
CBT triangle – choose a specific event/stressor • Thoughts (about self, others, the world in general) • Emotions • Behavior	
Evening routine – complete before midnight	
Empowering • "I am" poster (two minutes) with music **and** • Positive affirmations (three times) with music	
Somatic quieting • Progressive relaxation	

Day 4 – CBT triangle

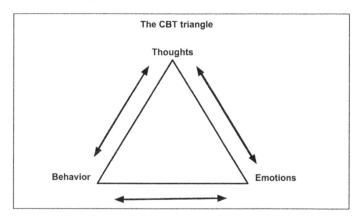

Event

_____

_____

Emotions

_____

_____

Thoughts

_____

_____

Behaviors

_____

_____

Day 5 – Cognitive distortions chart	Completed
Morning routine – complete before noon	
Nourishing and supporting your body • Vitamin supplement with B-complex vitamins **or** • Green smoothie **or** • Wheatgrass	
Empowering • "I am" poster (two minutes) with music **and** • Positive affirmations (three times) with music	
Building feelings of peace and safety • Create a virtual shield **or** • Loving-kindness meditation	
Daily action step – complete any time during the day	
Cognitive distortions chart	
Evening routine – complete before midnight	
Empowering • "I am" poster (two minutes) with music **and** • Positive affirmations (three times) with music	
Somatic quieting • Progressive relaxation	

Day 5 – Cognitive distortions chart

Personalization	The tendency to take everything very personally. This can either come in the form of assuming that something was intended as a personal attack, or it might manifest in a belief that everything that happened is all our fault. We're personally to blame for everything.
Selective attention/ mental filtering	The tendency to focus on negative events, while filtering out, or ignoring the positive events, or things that went well.
Fortune telling	A form of jumping to conclusions, where we assume we know what will happen in the future. Usually fortune telling includes pessimistic thinking, or what could go wrong.
Mind reading	Jumping to conclusions where we assume that we know what someone else is thinking. These conclusions are rarely, if ever, based on facts or concrete evidence, but rather based on personal feelings and opinions.
Catastrophizing	The tendency to blow circumstances out of proportion and make things out to be a lot worse than they should be; basically we're making mountains out of molehills.
Overgeneralization	To make broad generalizations that are based on a single event and minimal evidence. A clue that we might be using overgeneralization, is when we use phrases

	that include the words *never* or *always*. For example, "You always…" or "He never…"
Labeling	The tendency to make global statements about ourselves or others based on behavior in a specific situation. For example, "I'm a failure!" or, "You are an insensitive jerk." It changes a specific behavior or incident and turns it into an all-encompassing definition
Shoulding and musting	The tendency to make unrealistic and unreasonable demands on yourself and others. "I should have done this," or "She should have done that."
Emotional reasoning	The tendency to interpret our experience of reality based upon how we are feeling in the moment. Our emotional state skews our interpretation of the actual event.
Magnification and minimization	The tendency to magnify the positive attributes of another person, while minimizing our own positive attributes. We often compare someone else's highlight reel with our blooper reel. This devalues ourselves, while putting someone else on a pedestal.
Black and white/ all-or-none thinking	You are either a success or a failure. Your performance was totally good or totally bad. If you are not perfect, then you are a failure. This binary way of thinking leads to unreasonable expectations, and low self-esteem, and/or harsh criticism of others.

Event

_____

_____

_____

Thoughts

_____

_____

_____

Cognitive distortions

_____

_____

_____

Day 6 – Perfectionistic tendencies chart	Completed
Morning routine – complete before noon	
Nourishing and supporting your body • Vitamin supplement with B-complex vitamins **or** • Green smoothie **or** • Wheatgrass	
Empowering • "I am" poster (two minutes) with music **and** • Positive affirmations (three times) with music	
Building feelings of peace and safety • Create a virtual shield **or** • Loving-kindness meditation	
Daily action step – complete any time during the day	
Perfectionistic tendencies chart	
Evening routine – complete before midnight	
Empowering • "I am" poster (two minutes) with music **and** • Positive affirmations (three times) with music	
Somatic quieting • Progressive relaxation	

Day 6 – Perfectionistic tendencies chart

Perfectionism vs. Striving for excellence

Perfectionism	Striving for excellence
Unreasonably high expectations. Only two options: perfection (being without flaw) or failure.	High expectations. Follows a pattern of trying, making mistakes, and trying again.
Based on foundation of pride, self-doubt, and fear.	Based on foundation of confidence, courage, hope, hard work, and patience.
Stagnant. Wants to find a "perfect" spot and stay there.	Movement in a positive direction.
Uses social comparison to determine self-worth and to boost self-esteem.	Uses social comparison for self-evaluation and growth (role models).
Thoughts - "I'm not perfect so you can't be perfect either," or, "At least I'm better than you."	Thoughts - "How am I doing? Is there something I can learn or do better from watching what other people are doing? "
Emotions - Envy, coveting, jealousy, anger, resentment, blame, justification, judgmental, dissatisfaction, hatred, guilt, anxiety, failure	Emotions - Grateful, content, compassionate, inspired, or motivated to become better

Self-evaluation: I have perfectionistic tendencies

Evidence for	Evidence against

Day 7 – Connect with nature and/or exercise	Completed
Morning routine – complete before noon	
Nourishing and supporting your body • Vitamin supplement with B-complex vitamins **or** • Green smoothie **or** • Wheatgrass	
Empowering • "I am" poster (two minutes) with music **and** • Positive affirmations (three times) with music	
Building feelings of peace and safety • Create a virtual shield **or** • Loving-kindness meditation	
Daily action step – complete any time during the day	
Connect with nature and/or exercise (20-30 minutes)	
Evening routine – complete before midnight	
Empowering • "I am" poster (two minutes) with music **and** • Positive affirmations (three times) with music	
Somatic quieting • Progressive relaxation	

Day 7 – Connect with nature and/or exercise

Dedicate 20-30 minutes to calm the body and mind either by exercising, or by connecting with nature, and preferably by combining the two.

Virtually any form of exercise can act as a stress reliever, but activities such as walking or jogging that involve repetitive movements of large muscle groups can be particularly stress relieving, since they offer many of the same benefits as meditation.

Spending time in nature is good for the body and the mind. It helps relieve feelings of worry, anxiety, and stress, and contributes to your physical wellbeing by reducing blood rate, heart rate, muscle tension and the production of stress hormones. Allow yourself to be in the moment.

This activity will obviously vary depending on season, location, or current weather conditions. If you can't go outside and take a walk, then just adapt, and do the best you can. Be creative. What can you do to create an interaction with nature?

• Take a walk through some beautiful natural scenery whether that be in a park, along a beach, a river trail, a mountain path, or just around the neighborhood.

• Mall-walk or use a treadmill while listening to a recording of nature sounds.

• Groom a desktop Zen garden or executive sandbox.

Enjoy 30 minutes petting, playing with and interacting with your pet.

Day 8 – Discovering perceived rewards	Completed
Morning routine – complete before noon	
Nourishing and supporting your body • Vitamin supplement with B-complex vitamins **or** • Green smoothie **or** • Wheatgrass	
Empowering • "I am" poster (two minutes) with music **and** • Positive affirmations (three times) with music	
Building feelings of peace and safety • Create a virtual shield **or** • Loving-kindness meditation	
Daily action step – complete any time during the day	
Spend 20-30 minutes writing about one of more of the following prompts: • What would be the results if I stopped worrying, feeling anxious, stressed, and/or fearful? What would happen to me? What would happen to the people that I care about? • Do I feel that worrying about someone demonstrates my love and concern for that person?	
Evening routine – complete before midnight	
Empowering • "I am" poster (two minutes) with music **and** • Positive affirmations (three times) with music	
Somatic quieting • Progressive relaxation	

Day 8 – Discovering perceived rewards

Spend 20-30 minutes writing about one or more of the following prompts:

- What would be the results if I stopped worrying, feeling anxious, stressed, and/or fearful? What would happen to me? What would happen to the people that I care about?

- Do I feel that worrying about someone demonstrates my love and concern for that person?

- Do I feel guilty if I'm not constantly worrying, stressed or anxious?

- Did I grow up seeing a model of fear, anxiety, worry, and/or stress and assume that's the proper way to "adult"?

_____

_____

_____

_____

_____

_____

_____

_____

_____

_____

_____

_____

_____

_____

_____

_____

YOU GOT THIS!

Day 9 – Taking a deeper look at core beliefs	Completed
Morning routine – complete before noon	
Nourishing and supporting your body • Vitamin supplement with B-complex vitamins **or** • Green smoothie **or** • Wheatgrass	
Empowering • "I am" poster (two minutes) with music **and** • Positive affirmations (three times) with music	
Building feelings of peace and safety • Create a virtual shield **or** • Loving-kindness meditation	
Daily action step – complete any time during the day	
Spend 20-30 minutes journaling on one or more of the following prompts • My core beliefs about fear, anxiety, worry, and stress… • Those core beliefs came from… • My perceived rewards for fear, anxiety, worry, and stress are…	
Evening routine – complete before midnight	
Empowering • "I am" poster (two minutes) with music **and** • Positive affirmations (three times) with music	
Somatic quieting • Progressive relaxation	

Day 9 – Taking a deeper look at core beliefs

Spend 20-30 minutes writing about one or more of the following prompts:

- My core beliefs about fear, anxiety, worry, and stress are...

- Those core beliefs came from...

- My perceived rewards for fear, anxiety, worry, and stress are...

Day 10 – Visualization to let go of unnecessary burdens

Visualization exercise

The visualization exercise for today is to symbolically hand over our emotional burdens to our higher power. During this visualization, I'm going to use the pronouns "he and his" when referring to the higher power, but you could substitute the pronouns "she and her," or "it and its" if that feels more appropriate to you.

Take a few deep belly breaths and close your eyes to minimize distractions. I want you to visualize that you are hiking up a mountain trail. I want you to look around and notice as much detail as you can. What does the scenery look like? What kinds of trees do you see? Is the path steep, or is it a gentle incline? Is the sun shining, or is it stormy? Notice the time of day and the season. Notice any smells that might be there. Notice any sounds that you might hear. Notice your position on the trail; are you just starting at the bottom of the trail, nearing the top, or somewhere in the middle?

As you're walking along, you notice that something seems to be hampering your progress. Then you notice that you're carrying a bag, and inside this bag are rocks that symbolize your emotional burdens.

Now I want you to pay attention to the bag you are carrying. What kind of bag is it? Is it a backpack, or maybe a big sack like a pillowcase that you hold onto with your hand as it swings over one shoulder? What does it look like? Imagine the color, texture, and feel of the bag. What is it made out of? How big is it? How heavy is it? Is it nearly empty or bulging, stretching, and ready to burst the seams?

Now imagine the rocks inside the bag that represent those hurtful emotions that you're carrying. It might include feelings of worry, fear, anxiety, stress, anger, resentment, shame, abandonment, or betrayal. Or it might include something else that concerns a current situation, or perhaps an event that happened in the past, or even an anticipated event in the future. What do these rocks look like? What type of stone are they? Are they smooth or are they jagged? Describe the size, color, and shape of the rocks. How do you feel as you heft their weight in your bag? Is it easy, or are your legs buckling under the weight?

Now, pay attention to your pace as you continue up the trail. Are you running, skipping, walking, trudging, stumbling, or even crawling? How do you feel?

As you're traveling along the path, you turn and notice that someone is traveling beside you. Although you've never met this personage before, you recognize that it is your higher power. What does he look like? What does it feel like to be in his presence?

Your higher power has the ability to see through your bag, and is aware of each and every emotional burden you are carrying, as well as all the circumstances and events that caused them. He looks at you with compassion and empathy.

Now you feel an overwhelming sense of love and acceptance sweeping over you. This love is deep and intense. You feel it from the tip of your toes to the crown of your head. You accept this love and allow it to flow through you. You know, without a doubt, and perhaps for the first time, that your higher power cares deeply, personally, and intimately about you.

Your higher power calls you by name and offers to take your burdens. He is all powerful, and these burdens are light to him; in fact, he considers it a pleasure to be able to serve you. However, he will not force you against your will because he respects you too much to take away your agency.

What happens next? Do you accept his offer? Do you give him the whole bag, or do you sort through it and select just a few stones from inside the bag, and hand him those while choosing to keep the rest? What thoughts and feelings are going through your mind as you hand him the stones?

Whether you were willing to let go of all, some, or none of your stones, you see your higher power smile at you; and once again you feel that overwhelming feeling of love sweeping over you. He loves you if you keep your stones, and he loves you if you let them go. He honors your freedom to choose.

What happens next? What message does your higher power want to share with you? What encouragement does he give? What advice does he give?

It's time for him to go now, but your higher power is willing to come again and walk beside you. He's also willing to ease your burdens if you ask, believe that he'll take them, and be willing to let them go.

Notice your surroundings again. Pay attention to any changes that may have occurred. Is your bag any lighter? Does it take less effort as you hike up the trail? Notice your pace as you continue along the trail. Are you running, skipping, walking, trudging, stumbling, or even crawling? Is it any different from before? How do you feel?

Look around at the scenery, is it the same or has it changed as well? Look around and notice as much detail as you can. What kinds of trees do you see? Is the path steep, or is it a gentle incline? Is the sun shining, or is it stormy? Notice the quality of the light. Notice the time of day and the season. Notice any smells that might be there. Notice any sounds that you might hear.

Now it's time for you to return as well, but remember that you can return here any time that you want to. I want you to return your focus to your breathing. Take a few more breaths while you allow the vision to slowly fade, and you return to your natural surroundings.

Day 11 – Connect with nature and/or exercise	Completed
Morning routine – complete before noon	
Nourishing and supporting your body • Vitamin supplement with B-complex vitamins **or** • Green smoothie **or** • Wheatgrass	
Empowering • "I am" poster (two minutes) with music **and** • Positive affirmations (three times) with music	
Building feelings of peace and safety • Create a virtual shield **or** • Loving-kindness meditation	
Daily action step – complete any time during the day	
Connect with nature and/or exercise (20-30 minutes)	
Evening routine – complete before midnight	
Empowering • "I am" poster (two minutes) with music **and** • Positive affirmations (three times) with music	
Somatic quieting • Progressive relaxation	

Day 11 – Connect with nature and/or exercise

Dedicate 20-30 minutes to calm the body and mind either by exercising, or by connecting with nature, and preferably by combining the two.

Virtually any form of exercise can act as a stress reliever, but activities such as walking or jogging that involve repetitive movements of large muscle groups can be particularly stress relieving, since they offer many of the same benefits as meditation.

Spending time in nature is good for the body and the mind. It helps relieve feelings of worry, anxiety and stress, and contributes to your physical wellbeing by reducing blood rate, heart rate, muscle tension, and the production of stress hormones. Allow yourself to be in the moment.

This activity will obviously vary depending on season, location, or current weather conditions. If you can't go outside and take a walk, then just adapt, and do the best you can. Be creative. What can you do to create an interaction with nature?

- Take a walk through some beautiful natural scenery whether that be in a park, along a beach, a river trail, a mountain path, or just around the neighborhood.

- Mall-walk or use a treadmill while listening to a recording of nature sounds.

- Groom a desktop Zen garden or executive sandbox.

- Enjoy 30 minutes petting, playing with and interacting with your pet.

Day 12 – Core beliefs about self-worth and lovability	Completed
Morning routine – complete before noon	
Nourishing and supporting your body • Vitamin supplement with B-complex vitamins **or** • Green smoothie **or** • Wheatgrass	
Empowering • "I am" poster (two minutes) with music **and** • Positive affirmations (three times) with music	
Building feelings of peace and safety • Create a virtual shield **or** • Loving-kindness meditation	
Daily action step – complete any time during the day	
Spend 20-30 minutes journaling on one or more of the following prompts: • I have inherent value and lovability because… • I believe I only have worth and value if … • I believe I am only lovable if…	
Evening routine – complete before midnight	
Empowering • "I am" poster (two minutes) with music **and** • Positive affirmations (three times) with music	
Somatic quieting • Progressive relaxation	

Day 12 – Core beliefs about self-worth and lovability

Today's action step is to increase awareness about your perception of your lovability and self-worth, by looking deeper at your core values and beliefs. Spend 20-30 minutes writing about one or more of the following prompts:

- I have inherent value and lovability because...

- I believe I only have worth and value if ...

- I believe I am only lovable if...

- My beliefs about my value and lovability came from...

Day 13 – Evaluating threats to lovability

The action step for today is to analyze an event for source of threats. What was the event? What were your emotions? What were your thoughts?

Remember that fear based emotions like anxiety, worry, and stress can arise when we feel a real, or perceived, threat to either our physical safety, or our self-worth safety. Evaluate your thoughts and emotions listed on the chart; write the letters P or S to represent whether you think this was a threat to your physical safety (P) or your self-worth safety (S).

Event

_____

Emotions	P or S	Thoughts	P or S

Something to think about: Would any of those emotions or thoughts be different, if you had a firm and unshakable belief in your own inherent value?

Day 14 – Connect with nature and/or exercise	Completed
Morning routine – complete before noon	
Nourishing and supporting your body • Vitamin supplement with B-complex vitamins **or** • Green smoothie **or** • Wheatgrass	
Empowering • "I am" poster (two minutes) with music **and** • Positive affirmations (three times) with music	
Building feelings of peace and safety • Create a virtual shield **or** • Loving-kindness meditation	
Daily action step – complete any time during the day	
Connect with nature and/or exercise (20-30 minutes)	
Evening routine – complete before midnight	
Empowering • "I am" poster (two minutes) with music **and** • Positive affirmations (three times) with music	
Somatic quieting • Progressive relaxation	

Day 14 – Connect with nature and/or exercise

Dedicate 20-30 minutes to calm the body and mind either by exercising, or by connecting with nature, and preferably by combining the two.

Virtually any form of exercise can act as a stress reliever, but activities such as walking or jogging that involve repetitive movements of large muscle groups can be particularly stress relieving, since they offer many of the same benefits as meditation.

Spending time in nature is good for the body and the mind. It helps relieve feelings of worry, anxiety and stress, and contributes to your physical wellbeing by reducing blood rate, heart rate, muscle tension, and the production of stress hormones. Allow yourself to be in the moment.

This activity will obviously vary depending on season, location, or current weather conditions. If you can't go outside and take a walk, then just adapt, and do the best you can. Be creative. What can you do to create an interaction with nature?

• Take a walk through some beautiful natural scenery whether that be in a park, along a beach, a river trail, a mountain path, or just around the neighborhood.

• Mall-walk or use a treadmill while listening to a recording of nature sounds.

• Groom a desktop Zen garden or executive sandbox.

• Enjoy 30 minutes petting, playing with and interacting with your pet.

Day 15 – Alternate methods of showing love/ concern	Completed
Morning routine – complete before noon	
Nourishing and supporting your body • Vitamin supplement with B-complex vitamins **or** • Green smoothie **or** • Wheatgrass	
Empowering • "I am" poster (two minutes) with music **and** • Positive affirmations (three times) with music	
Building feelings of peace and safety • Create a virtual shield **or** • Do a loving-kindness meditation	
Daily action step – complete any time during the day	
Practicing alternate methods of showing love and concern • Loving-kindness meditation **or** • Creating a virtual shield	
Evening routine – complete before midnight	
Empowering • "I am" poster (two minutes) with music **and** • Positive affirmations (three times) with music	
Somatic quieting • Progressive relaxation	

Day 15 – Practicing alternate methods of showing love and concern

Practice alternate methods of showing love and concern through loving-kindness meditation, or by creating a virtual shield.

Loving-kindness meditation II

Sit upright in a comfortable chair with both feet flat on the floor, and your hands resting gently in your lap. Close your eyes to minimize distractions, and take a few deep, belly breaths. Just relax and focus on the gentle sensation of breathing in and out.

Now I want you to pick an image of a person, just a mental image of someone you care about. It can be whoever you like, and just imagine you're looking at that person. While you're focusing on that image, we're going to say a simple mantra, and I want you to imagine that you're saying it to that person.

"I care about you. I have confidence in you. I trust that you have the strength and wisdom to handle your challenges. I trust that your experiences will be perfect for you. I respect your agency, and I love you without reservation. May you be safe and happy." [*Repeat three times*]

Now I'd like you to change the image, and I want you to imagine you're looking in a mirror. So you're looking at yourself as you repeat this mantra. This is a message for you.

"I care about you. I have confidence in you. I trust that you have the strength and wisdom to handle your challenges. I trust that your experiences will be perfect for you. I respect your agency, and I love you without reservation. May you be safe and happy." [*Repeat three times*]

Bring your attention back to your breath. Take a few more deep breaths, then gently open your eyes.

Creating a virtual shield around people you care about

Sit upright in a comfortable chair with both feet flat on the floor, and your hands resting gently in your lap. Close your eyes to minimize distractions, and take a few deep belly breaths. Just relax and focus on the gentle sensation of breathing in and out.

Imagine, intend, and visualize, creating a shield or force field that completely surrounds your loved ones. Be creative and specific in imagining what it looks like, what color it is, how it feels inside. Notice the quality of the light, and any other specific details you can think of. Fill the space inside this shield or force field with love, confidence, hope, and peace. Imagine your loved one being enveloped with feelings of love and peace. Imagine that this shield is a protection for your loved one. They are safe. The shield is a filter, not a wall. Only those experiences that will be for your loved one's greater good can enter through this filter. Only those experiences that are perfect for them are allowed to enter. Everything is going to be okay. In the end, everything is going to be okay. Your loved one is surrounded and protected by love, and empowered by your trust and confidence in him or her.

Bring your attention back to your breath. Take a few more deep breaths, then gently open your eyes.

Day 16 – Finding meaning and purpose	Completed
Morning routine – complete before noon	
Nourishing and supporting your body • Vitamin supplement with B-complex vitamins **or** • Green smoothie **or** • Wheatgrass	
Empowering • "I am" poster (two minutes) with music **and** • Positive affirmations (three times) with music	
Building feelings of peace and safety • Create a virtual shield **or** • Loving-kindness meditation	
Daily action step – complete any time during the day	
Values clarification chart	
Evening routine – complete before midnight	
Empowering • "I am" poster (two minutes) with music **and** • Positive affirmations (three times) with music	
Somatic quieting • Progressive relaxation	

Day 16 – Finding meaning and purpose

Values Clarification Chart – Rate each item on a scale of 1-10

Values	Importance	Time/ resources	Difference
Marriage/ intimate relationship			
Parenting			
Family			
Social/ friendships			
Career			
Education/ growth			
Relaxation			
Spirituality			
Citizenship/ causes			
Health			
Other:			

Things to think about:

- What things do you value?

- What things bring feelings of meaning and purpose in your life?

- Are there any areas in your life that you value, but aren't spending a proportionate amount of time and energy caring for those things?

- Our values change during different phases of our lives, and as circumstances change. Feel free to re-evaluate your values by filling in a fresh chart whenever you choose

Day 17 – Finding meaning and purpose part 2	Completed
Morning routine – complete before noon	
Nourishing and supporting your body • Vitamin supplement with B-complex vitamins **or** • Green smoothie **or** • Wheatgrass	
Empowering • "I am" poster (two minutes) with music **and** • Positive affirmations (three times) with music	
Building feelings of peace and safety • Create a virtual shield **or** • Loving-kindness meditation	
Daily action step – complete any time during the day	
Spend 30 minutes doing something that brings meaning and purpose into your life.	
Evening routine – complete before midnight	
Empowering • "I am" poster (two minutes) with music **and** • Positive affirmations (three times) with music	
Somatic quieting • Progressive relaxation	

Day 18 – Finding joy	Completed
Morning routine – complete before noon	
Nourishing and supporting your body • Vitamin supplement with B-complex vitamins **or** • Green smoothie **or** • Wheatgrass	
Empowering • "I am" poster (two minutes) with music **and** • Positive affirmations (three times) with music	
Building feelings of peace and safety • Create a virtual shield **or** • Loving-kindness meditation	
Daily action step – complete any time during the day	
Spend 20-30 minutes writing about one or more of the following prompts: • Things that bring me joy… • What kinds of activities did I used to find enjoyable, but haven't done for a while? • My core beliefs about hobbies and leisure activities are… • I learned these beliefs from…	
Evening routine – complete before midnight	
Empowering • "I am" poster (two minutes) with music **and** • Positive affirmations (three times) with music	
Somatic quieting • Progressive relaxation	

Day 18 – Finding joy

Today's action step is a journaling exercise. What brings you joy? First, list as many things as you can think of that bring you joy, or have brought you joy in the past. For example: scrapbooking, painting, playing a musical instrument, sewing, knitting, sports, yoga, meeting a friend for lunch, reading, writing, walking, cycling, making jewelry, sketching, writing poetry, working in the garden, etc.

Second, think about your core beliefs about joy, recreation, leisure, and laughter. Do you allow yourself to do those things, or are there beliefs that you're supposed to outgrow these activities, or perhaps they're a waste of time, and you're supposed to be doing more productive things?

Please spend 20-30 minutes writing about one or more of the following prompts:

• Things that bring me joy…

• What kinds of activities did I used to find enjoyable, but haven't done for a while?

• My core beliefs about hobbies and leisure activities are…

• I learned these beliefs from…

YOU GOT THIS!

Day 19 – Finding joy part 2	Completed
Morning routine – complete before noon	
Nourishing and supporting your body • Vitamin supplement with B-complex vitamins **or** • Green smoothie **or** • Wheatgrass	
Empowering • "I am" poster (two minutes) with music **and** • Positive affirmations (three times) with music	
Building feelings of peace and safety • Create a virtual shield **or** • Loving-kindness meditation	
Daily action step – complete any time during the day	
Spend 30 minutes doing something that brings you joy.	
Evening routine – complete before midnight	
Empowering • "I am" poster (two minutes) with music **and** • Positive affirmations (three times) with music	
Somatic quieting • Progressive relaxation	

Day 20 – Gratitude	Completed
Morning routine – complete before noon	
Nourishing and supporting your body • Vitamin supplement with B-complex vitamins **or** • Green smoothie **or** • Wheatgrass	
Empowering • "I am" poster (two minutes) with music **and** • Positive affirmations (three times) with music	
Building feelings of peace and safety • Create a virtual shield **or** • Loving-kindness meditation	
Daily action step – complete any time during the day	
List at least 100 things that you're grateful for.	
Evening routine – complete before midnight	
Empowering • "I am" poster (two minutes) with music **and** • Positive affirmations (three times) with music	
Somatic quieting • Progressive relaxation	

Day 20 – Gratitude

List at least 100 things that you're grateful for

_____

_____

_____

_____

_____

_____

_____

_____

_____

_____

_____

_____

_____

_____

_____

_____

_____

_____

_____

_____

_____

_____

_____

_____

YOU GOT THIS!

_____
_____
_____
_____
_____
_____
_____
_____
_____
_____
_____
_____
_____
_____
_____
_____
_____
_____
_____
_____
_____
_____
_____
_____
_____
_____

Day 21 – The healing power of forgiveness	Completed
Morning routine – complete before noon	
Nourishing and supporting your body • Vitamin supplement with B-complex vitamins **or** • Green smoothie **or** • Wheatgrass	
Empowering • "I am" poster (two minutes) with music **and** • Positive affirmations (three times) with music	
Building feelings of peace and safety • Create a virtual shield **or** • Loving-kindness meditation	
Daily action step – complete any time during the day	
The healing power of forgiveness journaling exercise • Core beliefs about forgiveness **or** • Self-forgiveness visualization exercise	
Evening routine – complete before midnight	
Empowering • "I am" poster (two minutes) with music **and** • Positive affirmations (three times) with music	
Somatic quieting • Progressive relaxation	

Day 21 – The healing power of forgiveness

Today's action step is a journaling exercise to increase awareness of your core beliefs about forgiveness, or to do a visualization exercise. Spend 20-30 minutes writing about one or more of the following prompts:

- If I forgive someone, that means…

- I don't want to forgive others because…

- I don't want to forgive myself because…

- Forgiving others or myself might reduce my stress because…

- I used to think forgiveness meant…, but now I believe it means…

Alternate activity - self forgiveness visualization exercise

Sometimes a person is willing to forgive others, but is unwilling to forgive themselves. They feel like they deserve to suffer, and forgiving themselves would be unjust. The same principles apply to forgiving yourself as forgiving other people. Remember that psychologists generally define forgiveness as a conscious, deliberate decision to release feelings of resentment or vengeance toward a person whether or not they actually deserve your forgiveness. An alternate activity to the journaling exercise, is to visualize yourself in a scenario, similar to the one described by Corrie Ten Boom when she met her former guard, only this time it is you facing yourself in the mirror. You know your past, just like Corrie knew the guard's past. Will you choose to lift your hand and touch the hand in the mirror?

Day 22 – Relationship stress	Completed
Morning routine – complete before noon	
Nourishing and supporting your body • Vitamin supplement with B-complex vitamins **or** • Green smoothie **or** • Wheatgrass	
Empowering • "I am" poster (two minutes) with music **and** • Positive affirmations (three times) with music	
Building feelings of peace and safety • Create a virtual shield **or** • Loving-kindness meditation	
Daily action step – complete any time during the day	
Virtual conversation	
Evening routine – complete before midnight	
Empowering • "I am" poster (two minutes) with music **and** • Positive affirmations (three times) with music	
Somatic quieting • Progressive relaxation	

Day 22 – Virtual conversation - Action step instructions

A virtual conversation is similar to some of the other visualization techniques we've tried, but with a few key components. First, you visualize the other person standing in front of you; second, you dump and let them have it; and third, you say you're sorry and ask for forgiveness (don't leave out the third step!)

1. The first step is to visualize the person or the person's "higher self" standing in front of you. It's very important to clarify that the person that you're having this conversation with is *not* in the room with you. You are by yourself. Under normal circumstances, yelling at people, and telling them off, doesn't improve relationships, but the imagined virtual being can handle it just fine. In actuality, you might be speaking to a tree, or a chair, or a steering wheel in the car; but you visualize the person standing in front of you, and you imagine asking for their permission to talk to them.

2. The second step is to let them have it. Tell them all the things you've been holding back. You might even be yelling and swearing, and that's a good thing. Just get it all out. When you can't think of anything else to say, then it's time for the final step.

3. The third and final step is to apologize to this person for feeling all those negative thoughts and emotions towards them, and ask for forgiveness for anything you may have done that harmed them. Apologizing brings healing.

Some people don't want to do the third step. "But it's not my fault, I didn't do anything wrong, it was all the other guy," they will say. Sometimes, that may be true, such as in the story of Corrie Ten Boom. She was an innocent victim, what could she possibly apologize for? She could express remorse for her negative feelings. Saying, "I'm sorry for my unkind feelings," is a way of acknowledging that you have those feelings, which is a necessary step in letting them go. This brings healing and closure.

Day 23 – Connect with nature and/or exercise	Completed
Morning routine – complete before noon	
Nourishing and supporting your body • Vitamin supplement with B-complex vitamins **or** • Green smoothie **or** • Wheatgrass	
Empowering • "I am" poster (two minutes) with music **and** • Positive affirmations (three times) with music	
Building feelings of peace and safety • Create a virtual shield **or** • Loving-kindness meditation	
Daily action step – complete any time during the day	
Connect with nature and/or exercise (20-30 minutes)	
Evening routine – complete before midnight	
Empowering • "I am" poster (two minutes) with music **and** • Positive affirmations (three times) with music	
Somatic quieting • Progressive relaxation	

Day 23 – Connect with nature and/or exercise

Dedicate 20-30 minutes to calm the body and mind either by exercising, or by connecting with nature, and preferably by combining the two.

Virtually any form of exercise can act as a stress reliever, but activities such as walking or jogging that involve repetitive movements of large muscle groups can be particularly stress relieving, since they offer many of the same benefits as meditation.

Spending time in nature is good for the body and the mind. It helps relieve feelings of worry, anxiety, and stress, and contributes to your physical wellbeing by reducing blood rate, heart rate, muscle tension, and the production of stress hormones. Allow yourself to be in the moment.

This activity will obviously vary depending on season, location, or current weather conditions. If you can't go outside and take a walk, then just adapt, and do the best you can. Be creative. What can you do to create an interaction with nature?

• Take a walk through some beautiful natural scenery whether that be in a park, along a beach, a river trail, a mountain path, or just around the neighborhood.

• Mall-walk or use a treadmill while listening to a recording of nature sounds.

• Groom a desktop Zen garden or executive sandbox.

• Enjoy 30 minutes petting, playing with and interacting with your pet.

Day 24 – Social support network diagram	Completed
Morning routine – complete before noon	
Nourishing and supporting your body • Vitamin supplement with B-complex vitamins **or** • Green smoothie **or** • Wheatgrass	
Empowering • "I am" poster (two minutes) with music **and** • Positive affirmations (three times) with music	
Building feelings of peace and safety • Create a virtual shield **or** • Loving-kindness meditation	
Daily action step – complete any time during the day	
Social support network diagram and assessment	
Evening routine – complete before midnight	
Empowering • "I am" poster (two minutes) with music **and** • Positive affirmations (three times) with music	
Somatic quieting • Progressive relaxation	

Day 24 – Social support diagram - Action step instructions

We're going to visually represent the resources in your support network with a diagram that looks something like a solar system, with your name in the center and a few concentric rings. We're going to write in the names of friends, family members, significant others, as well as other resources including church, community, and government resources on the diagram. Those people and resources that you feel close to you, will be listed within the inner circle. Those that you are a little less comfortable with, are placed in the outer circle. And those resources that exist, but you aren't likely to ask for help can be outside the rings somewhere.

After listing these people and resources, I want you to think about what kind of support they might be able to provide. Can they help with emotional support, informational support, or practical support? On the chart place a letter E - emotional, I - informational, or P - practical next to each of the resources.

<u>Emotional support</u> is someone with a listening ear, who will show compassion and empathy.

<u>Informational support</u> is someone who can give good advice, or help you work through your problems.

<u>Practical support</u> is tangible, or includes an action of some kind.

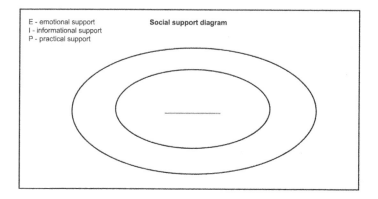

Day 25 – Finding solutions – part 1	Completed
Morning routine – complete before noon	
Nourishing and supporting your body • Vitamin supplement with B-complex vitamins **or** • Green smoothie **or** • Wheatgrass	
Empowering • "I am" poster (two minutes) with music **and** • Positive affirmations (three times) with music	
Building feelings of peace and safety • Create a virtual shield **or** • Loving-kindness meditation	
Daily action step – complete any time during the day	
Finding solutions chart with self-recommendations	
Evening routine – complete before midnight	
Empowering • "I am" poster (two minutes) with music **and** • Positive affirmations (three times) with music	
Somatic quieting • Progressive relaxation	

Day 25 – Finding solutions - part 1

The purpose for the action step today is to begin looking for answers to your problems. Remember that you are the expert on you and your situation. Chances are that you already have many of the answers already inside of you. One way to see that you really do have solutions inside you, is to pretend that you're giving advice to someone else.

To fill out this chart, list a stressful event or situation, as well as any thoughts and emotions relating to that event. Look to see if there are any automatic thoughts and cognitive distortions like: personalization, selective attention/mental filtering, fortune telling, mind reading, catastrophizing, overgeneralization, labeling, shoulding and musting, emotional reasoning, magnification and minimization, black and white/all-or-nothing thinking (aka perfectionism). The final column is self-advice. If this were a friend coming to you for advice, what would you recommend?

Finding solutions - self recommendations

Event	Thoughts	Recommendations
Emotions	Cognitive distortions?	

Day 26 – Finding solutions – health related stress	Completed
Morning routine – complete before noon	
Nourishing and supporting your body • Vitamin supplement with B-complex vitamins **or** • Green smoothie **or** • Wheatgrass	
Empowering • "I am" poster (two minutes) with music **and** • Positive affirmations (three times) with music	
Building feelings of peace and safety • Create a virtual shield **or** • Loving-kindness meditation	
Daily action step – complete any time during the day	
Finding solutions chart with self-recommendations • Health related stress	
Evening routine – complete before midnight	
Empowering • "I am" poster (two minutes) with music **and** • Positive affirmations (three times) with music	
Somatic quieting • Progressive relaxation	

Day 26 – Finding solutions - health related stress

Our physical health influences every aspect of our lives. Do you have any concerns about your health? Start with the basic questions: How bad is this? Can I survive this? Is it permanent? Is it temporary? Can I put it into perspective?

If you're enjoying good or moderate health, perhaps health stress is just taking preventative measures, or doing something to boost energy.

If you're dealing with a chronic illness, then evaluating a social support diagram might be helpful, or working on finding meaning and purpose, or increasing the positive feelings of gratitude. You are the expert on your situation.

Finding solutions - self recommendations

Event	Thoughts	Recommendations
Emotions	Cognitive distortions?	

Day 27 – Connect with nature and/or exercise	Completed
Morning routine – complete before noon	
Nourishing and supporting your body • Vitamin supplement with B-complex vitamins **or** • Green smoothie **or** • Wheatgrass	
Empowering • "I am" poster (two minutes) with music **and** • Positive affirmations (three times) with music	
Building feelings of peace and safety • Create a virtual shield **or** • Loving-kindness meditation	
Daily action step – complete any time during the day	
Connect with nature and/or exercise (20-30 minutes)	
Evening routine – complete before midnight	
Empowering • "I am" poster (two minutes) with music **and** • Positive affirmations (three times) with music	
Somatic quieting • Progressive relaxation	

Day 27 – Connect with nature and/or exercise

Dedicate 20-30 minutes to calm the body and mind either by exercising, or by connecting with nature, and preferably by combining the two.

Virtually any form of exercise can act as a stress reliever, but activities such as walking or jogging that involve repetitive movements of large muscle groups can be particularly stress relieving, since they offer many of the same benefits as meditation.

Spending time in nature is good for the body and the mind. It helps relieve feelings of worry, anxiety, and stress, and contributes to your physical wellbeing by reducing blood rate, heart rate, muscle tension, and the production of stress hormones. Allow yourself to be in the moment.

This activity will obviously vary depending on season, location, or current weather conditions. If you can't go outside and take a walk, then just adapt, and do the best you can. Be creative. What can you do to create an interaction with nature?

• Take a walk through some beautiful natural scenery whether that be in a park, along a beach, a river trail, a mountain path, or just around the neighborhood.

• Mall-walk or use a treadmill while listening to a recording of nature sounds.

• Groom a desktop Zen garden or executive sandbox.

• Enjoy 30 minutes petting, playing with and interacting with your pet.

Day 28 – Finding solutions – work related stress	Completed
Morning routine – complete before noon	
Nourishing and supporting your body • Vitamin supplement with B-complex vitamins **or** • Green smoothie **or** • Wheatgrass	
Empowering • "I am" poster (two minutes) with music **and** • Positive affirmations (three times) with music	
Building feelings of peace and safety • Create a virtual shield **or** • Loving-kindness meditation	
Daily action step – complete any time during the day	
Finding solutions chart with self-recommendations • Work related stress	
Evening routine – complete before midnight	
Empowering • "I am" poster (two minutes) with music **and** • Positive affirmations (three times) with music	
Somatic quieting • Progressive relaxation	

Day 28 – Finding solutions – work related stress

We spend a lot of time at work. What can we do to reduce work related stress?

We've discussed many tools to cope with stress such as exercise, somatic quieting, and becoming aware of cognitive distortions. Other ideas to reduce stress at work include: clarifying expectations, staying organized, improving physical comfort, chunking rather than multitasking, striving for excellence while avoiding perfectionism, walking during lunch breaks, avoiding interpersonal conflict, strengthening conflict resolution skills, and even the idea of taking a vacation.

If you've done everything, and you still are stressed by a toxic job or a toxic boss; then step back and take a critical look at whether or not you need to find the courage to end a job, and move on somewhere else. Money isn't everything. You're allowed to prioritize happiness. What do you want most? You are the expert on you.

Finding solutions - self recommendations

Event	Thoughts	Recommendations
Emotions	Cognitive distortions?	

Day 29 – Core beliefs about money	Completed
Morning routine – complete before noon	
Nourishing and supporting your body • Vitamin supplement with B-complex vitamins **or** • Green smoothie **or** • Wheatgrass	
Empowering • "I am" poster (two minutes) with music **and** • Positive affirmations (three times) with music	
Building feelings of peace and safety • Create a virtual shield **or** • Loving-kindness meditation	
Daily action step – complete any time during the day	
Spend 20-30 minutes journaling on one or more of the following prompts: • What are your current "money scripts" or financial belief patterns? • Where did those core beliefs about money come from?	
Evening routine – complete before midnight	
Empowering • "I am" poster (two minutes) with music **and** • Positive affirmations (three times) with music	
Somatic quieting • Progressive relaxation	

Day 29 – Core beliefs about money

Financial matters often are a source of fear, anxiety, worry, and stress. Today's action step is to increase your awareness about your core beliefs about money.

We've already investigated how hidden core beliefs about worry and forgiveness may keep us from letting go of some of our burdens, in a similar fashion our unconscious core beliefs about money may contribute to some of our worries and frustrations about money and wealth. Your core beliefs about money might be called your "money script." Money scripts are the unconscious beliefs about money that are often learned in childhood, and passed down from generation to generation. Research shows that our unconscious money scripts have been found to be associated with our income, net worth, credit card and other debt, financial outcomes, financial behaviors, and other aspects of financial health.

Four of the basic core money beliefs are money avoidance, money worship, money status, and money vigilance. We may carry beliefs from more than one category, even when the categories seem to contradict each other.

Spend 20-30 minutes journaling on one of more of the following prompts:

• What are your current "money scripts" or financial belief patterns?

• Where did those core beliefs about money come from?

• Do your money beliefs support your life goals, or are they creating a roadblock?

_____

_____

_____

_____

_____

_____

YOU GOT THIS!

Something to think about: Money scripts are unconscious beliefs about money, and they are usually formed in childhood.   As an adult, you have the opportunity to change those beliefs and create new patterns.   In actuality, money is neither good nor bad, it is neutral.   What makes money "good" or "bad" is our attitude towards it, how we earned it, and/or how we choose to spend it.

Day 30 – Finding solutions – money related stress	Completed
Morning routine – complete before noon	
Nourishing and supporting your body • Vitamin supplement with B-complex vitamins **or** • Green smoothie **or** • Wheatgrass	
Empowering • "I am" poster (two minutes) with music **and** • Positive affirmations (three times) with music	
Building feelings of peace and safety • Create a virtual shield **or** • Loving-kindness meditation	
Daily action step – complete any time during the day	
Finding solutions chart with self-recommendations • money related stress	
Evening routine – complete before midnight	
Empowering • "I am" poster (two minutes) with music **and** • Positive affirmations (three times) with music	
Somatic quieting • Progressive relaxation	

Day 30 – Finding solutions - money related stress

Today's action step is to begin looking for solutions to any stressors relating to money. Becoming aware is the first step to empower yourself to make any necessary changes. Hopefully, the journaling exercise from yesterday helped you become aware of your core beliefs about money. Remember that our thoughts, our emotions, and our behaviors/actions are highly interconnected. Improving financial health requires changes in behavior, but those changes aren't likely to take place if they're not in line with your emotions and thoughts regarding money. Money scripts are unconscious beliefs about money, and they usually are formed in childhood. As an adult, you have the opportunity to change those beliefs, and create new patterns.

You may also choose to change your behaviors about money. Some recommendations include: avoiding and paying off debt, saving for emergencies, and planning and investing for retirement.

Finding solutions - self recommendations

Event	Thoughts	Recommendations
Emotions	Cognitive distortions?	

APPENDIX F

REFERENCES

Advocate Aurora Health. "How Exercise Can Build Your Confidence." *Health Enews*, Advocate Aurora Health, 24 July 2014, www.ahchealthenews.com/2014/07/24/how-exercise-can-build-your-confidence/.[49, 142]

Alberini, Cristina M. "Memory Reconsolidation." *Science Direct*, Elsevier Inc., 2013, www.sciencedirect.com/topics/neuroscience/memory-reconsolidation.[134]

Alcohol Rehab. "Higher Power in AA." *Drug and Alcohol Rehab Information and Resources - Alcohol Rehab*, 30 Oct. 2019, alcoholrehab.com/alcoholism/higher-power-in-aa/%C2%A0.[170, 171]

Allen, Karen, et al. "Pet Ownership, but Not ACE Inhibitor Therapy, Blunts Home Blood Pressure Responses to Mental Stress." *Hypertension*, 1 Apr. 2018, www.ahajournals.org/doi/full/10.1161/hyp.38.4.815.[67]

American Heart Association. "3 Tips to Manage Stress." *Www.heart.org*, June 2014, www.heart.org/en/healthy-living/healthy-lifestyle/stress-management/3-tips-to-manage-stress.[182]

American Psychological Association. "Stress in the Workplace." *American Psychological Association*, Mar. 2011, www.apa.org/news/press/releases/phwa-survey-summary.pdf.[206]

American Psychological Association. "What Is Cognitive Behavioral Therapy?" *American Psychological Association*, 2020, www.apa.org/ptsd-guideline/patients-and-families/cognitive-behavioral%C2%A0%C2%A0.[152]

Anxiety and Depression Association of America. "Facts & Statistics." *Anxiety and Depression Association of America, ADAA*, ADAA, 2020, adaa.org/about-adaa/press-room/facts-statistics.[14, 16]

APA Dictionary of Psychology. "Social Comparison Theory." *American Psychological Association*, 2020, dictionary.apa.org/social-comparison-theory.[160]

APA Dictionary of Psychology. "Yerkes-Dodson Law." *APA Dictionary of Psychology*, American Psychological Association, 2020, dictionary.apa.org/yerkes-dodson-law.[10]

Association for Psychological Science. "APS Registered Replication Report Project to Explore the 'Facial Feedback Hypothesis.'" *Association for Psychological Science - APS*, 2 Mar. 2015, www.psychologicalscience.org/publications/observer/obsonline/aps-registered-replication-report-project-to-explore-the-facial-feedback-hypothesis.html.[40]

BBC News. "SCI/TECH | Music Lovers 'Have Fish to Thank'." *BBC News*, BBC, 17 Feb. 2000, news.bbc.co.uk/2/hi/science/nature/645578.stm.[33]

Beckers, Tom, and Merel Kindt. "Memory Reconsolidation Interference as an Emerging Treatment for Emotional Disorders: Strengths, Limitations, Challenges, and Opportunities." *Annual Review of Clinical Psychology*, U.S. National Library of Medicine, 8 May 2017, www.ncbi.nlm.nih.gov/pmc/articles/PMC5424072/%C2%A0%C2%A0.[135]

Bellum, Sara. "Energy Drinks: A Boost in the Wrong Direction?" *The National Institute on Drug Abuse Blog* , National Institutes of Health, 2 May 2010, teens.drugabuse.gov/blog/post/energy-drinks-boost-wrong-direction.[73]

Benson, Herbert. "About Us - Dr. Herbert Benson - Benson-Henry Institute." *Benson-Henry Institute*, 2020, www.bensonhenryinstitute.org/about-us-dr-herbert-benson/.[20]

Bergland, Christopher. "Holding a Grudge Produces Cortisol and Diminishes Oxytocin." *Psychology Today*, Sussex Publishers, 11 Apr. 2015, www.psychologytoday.com/us/blog/the-athletes-way/201504/holding-grudge-produces-cortisol-and-diminishes-oxytocin.[198]

Bergland, Christopher. "The Brain Mechanics of Rumination and Repetitive Thinking." *Psychology Today*, Sussex Publishers, 1 Aug. 2015, www.psychologytoday.com/us/blog/the-athletes-way/201508/the-brain-mechanics-rumination-and-repetitive-thinking.[54]

Berkeley University of California. "What Is Forgiveness?" *Greater Good Magazine*, Berkeley University of California, 2020, greatergood.berkeley.edu/topic/forgiveness/definition.[193, 194]

Bjork, Linda. "17 Simple Ways to Relieve Worry, Stress, and Anxiety." *Hope for Healing*, 28 Dec. 2019, hopeforhealingfoundation.org/17-simple-ways-to-relieve-worry-stress-and-anxiety/.[180]

Bjork, Linda. "Emotional First Aid Kit." *Hope for Healing*, 19 Feb. 2020, hopeforhealingfoundation.org/emotional-first-aid-kit/.[28]

Bjork, Linda. "What to Do When You Hit an Emotional Wall." *Hope for Healing*, 19 Feb. 2020, hopeforhealingfoundation.org/what-to-do-when-you-hit-an-emotional-wall/.[31, 116]

Bjork, Linda. "Why Do We Compare Ourselves with Others?" *Two Good Things*, 1 Apr. 2020, www.twogoodthings.net/2020/01/10/why-do-we-compare-ourselves-with-others/. [156, 157, 165]

Bjork, Linda. *Crushed*. Amazon Kindle Direct Publishing, 2018.[27]

Boccia, Maddalena, et al. "The Meditative Mind: A Comprehensive Meta-Analysis of MRI Studies." *BioMed Research International*, Hindawi Publishing Corporation, 2015, www.ncbi.nlm.nih.gov/pmc/articles/PMC4471247/.[58]

Body, Dyvonne. "The Burden of Debt on Mental and Physical Health." *The Aspen Institute*, 2 Aug. 2018, www.aspeninstitute.org/blog-posts/hidden-costs-of-consumer-debt/.[217]

Bonfil, Albert. "Recognizing Cognitive Distortions: All-or-Nothing Thinking." *Cognitive Behavioral Therapy Los Angeles*, Cognitive Behavioral Therapy Los Angeles, 15 Apr. 2015, cogbtherapy.com/cbt-blog/cognitive-distortions-all-or-nothing-thinking.[155]

Borah, Mukundam, et al. "A Study of the Protective Effect of Triticum Aestivum L. in an Experimental Animal Model of Chronic Fatigue Syndrome." *Pharmacognosy Research*, Medknow Publications & Media Pvt Ltd, Oct. 2014, www.ncbi.nlm.nih.gov/pmc/articles/PMC4166815/.[82]

Braam, W, et al. "Loss of Response to Melatonin Treatment Is Associated with Slow Melatonin Metabolism." *Journal of Intellectual Disability Research: JIDR*, U.S. National Library of Medicine, June 2010, www.ncbi.nlm.nih.gov/pubmed/20576063.[112]

Brothen, Thomas. "What Ever Happened to John Dodson?" *American Psychological Association*, American Psychological Association, 2012, psycnet.apa.org/record/2011-17149-001.[12]

Brown, Brené. "The Power of Vulnerability." *TED*, TEDxHouston, June 2010, www.ted.com/talks/brene_brown_the_power_of_vulnerability?language=en.[174]

Buchanan, Tony W. "Retrieval of Emotional Memories." *Psychological Bulletin*, U.S. National Library of Medicine, Sept. 2007, www.ncbi.nlm.nih.gov/pmc/articles/PMC2265099/.[132]

Carr, Michelle. "Dream Deprived: A Modern Epidemic?" *Psychology Today*, 22 Aug. 2017, www.psychologytoday.com/us/blog/dream-factory/201708/dream-deprived-modern-epidemic.[106]

Centers for Disease Control and Prevention. "CDC - Sleep Hygiene Tips - Sleep and Sleep Disorders." *Centers for Disease Control and Prevention*, U.S. Department of Health & Human Services, 15 July 2016, www.cdc.gov/sleep/about_sleep/sleep_hygiene.html.[121]

Chen, Lung Hung, and Chia-Huei Wu. "Gratitude Enhances Change in Athletes' Self-Esteem: The Moderating Role of Trust in Coach." *Taylor & Francis*, 8 May 2014, www.tandfonline.com/doi/abs/10.1080/10413200.2014.889255.[184]

Cherry, Kendra. "Robert Yerkes Was Influential in Comparative Psychology." *Verywell Mind*, 13 Apr. 2020, www.verywellmind.com/robert-yerkes-biography-2795531.[11]

Cherry, Kendra. "Why Optimal Arousal Levels Lead to Better Athletic Performance." *Verywell Mind*, 6 Jan. 2020, www.verywellmind.com/what-is-the-yerkes-dodson-law-2796027.[8,9]

Chu, Kathryn. "This Is My Go-To Recipe When My Anxiety Spikes." *Healthline*, 28 June 2019, www.healthline.com/health/mental-health/green-smoothie-anxiety#1.[80]

Colier, Nancy. "Why We Hold Grudges, and How to Let Them Go." *Psychology Today*, Sussex Publishers, 4 Mar. 2015, www.psychologytoday.com/us/blog/inviting-monkey-tea/201503/why-we-hold-grudges-and-how-let-them-go.[196]

Columbia University. "First World Happiness Report Launched at the United Nations." *Earth Institute*, Columbia University, 2 Apr. 2012, www.earth.columbia.edu/articles/view/2960%C2%A0.[93, 94]

Corliss, Julie. "Mindfulness Meditation May Ease Anxiety, Mental Stress." *Harvard Health Blog*, Harvard University, 5 Aug. 2019, www.health.harvard.edu/blog/mindfulness-meditation-may-ease-anxiety-mental-stress-201401086967.[137]

Crichton-Stuart, Cathleen. "9 Foods That Help Reduce Anxiety." *Medical News Today*, MediLexicon International, 1 Aug. 2018, www.medicalnewstoday.com/articles/322652#nine-foods-to-eat-to-help-reduce-anxiety.[79]

Cronkleton, Emily. "Wheatgrass Benefits: 11 Reasons to Enjoy." *Healthline*, 5 May 2017, www.healthline.com/health/food-nutrition/wheatgrass-benefits.[81]

Cuddy, Amy J.C., et al. "The Benefit of Power Posing Before a High-Stakes Social Evaluation." *Harvard Business School*, Harvard Library Office for Scholarly Communication, Sept. 2012, dash.harvard.edu/bitstream/handle/1/9547823/13-027.pdf?sequence=1%3E.%5B43.[42]

Cuncic, Arlin. "An Overview of Viktor Frankl's Logotherapy." *Very Well Mind*, 6 Oct. 2019, www.verywellmind.com/an-overview-of-victor-frankl-s-logotherapy-4159308.[177]

Davis, Joshua Ian, et al. "How Does Facial Feedback Modulate Emotional Experience?" *National Center for Biotechnology Information*, U.S. National

Library of Medicine, 1 Oct. 2009,
www.ncbi.nlm.nih.gov/pmc/articles/PMC2764988/.[36]

Davis, Soph Sam. "4 Sets of Somatic Mindfulness Exercises for People Who Have Experienced Trauma." *Psych Central*, 8 Oct. 2018, psychcentral.com/lib/4-sets-of-somatic-mindfulness-exercises-for-people-who-have-experienced-trauma/.[99]

De Moor, M.H.M., et al. "Regular Exercise, Anxiety, Depression and Personality: A Population-Based Study." *Preventive Medicine*, Academic Press, 24 Jan. 2006, www.sciencedirect.com/science/article/pii/S0091743505002331.[50, 139]

Department of Health & Human Services, State Government of Victoria, Australia. "Vitamin B." *Better Health Channel*, Department of Health & Human Services, 31 May 2014, www.betterhealth.vic.gov.au/health/healthyliving/vitamin-b%C2%A0%C2%A0.[75]

Dictionary.com. "Intrinsic." *Dictionary.com*, 2020, www.dictionary.com/browse/intrinsic.[172]

Diffen. "Parasympathetic vs Sympathetic Nervous System." *Diffen*, 2020, www.diffen.com/difference/Parasympathetic_nervous_system_vs_Sympathetic_nervous_system.[17]

DiSalvo, David. "Your Brain Sees Even When You Don't." *Forbes*, Forbes Magazine, 23 June 2013, www.forbes.com/sites/daviddisalvo/2013/06/22/your-brain-sees-even-when-you-dont/#2f78aa2716a.[25]

Ekman, Paul. "Darwin's Contributions to Our Understanding of Emotional Expressions." *Philosophical Transactions of the Royal Society of London. Series B, Biological Sciences*, The Royal Society, 12 Dec. 2009, www.ncbi.nlm.nih.gov/pmc/articles/PMC2781895/.[38]

Encyclopaedia Britannica. "John Gardner." *Encyclopaedia Britannica*, 2020, Encyclopaedia Britannica.[178]

Famous Psychologists. "Leon Festinger." *Famous Psychologists*, 2020,
www.famouspsychologists.org/leon-festinger/%C2%A0.[158]

Felson, Sabrina. "Stages of Sleep: REM and Non-REM Sleep Cycles." *WebMD*,
WebMD, 26 Oct. 2018, www.webmd.com/sleep-disorders/sleep-101.[102]

Fillon, Mike. "Holding a Grudge Can Be Bad for Your Health." *WebMD*,
WebMD, 25 Feb. 2000,
www.webmd.com/depression/news/20000225/holding-a-grudge-can-be-
bad-for-your-health#1.[197]

Ford, Julian. "Did You Know Your Brain Has an Alarm?" *Psychology Today*,
Sussex Publishers, 31 Jan. 2013,
www.psychologytoday.com/us/blog/hijacked-your-brain/201301/did-you-
know-your-brain-has-alarm.[6]

Franklin Covey. "Habit 2: Begin with the End in Mind." *Franklin Covey*, 2020,
www.franklincovey.com/the-7-habits/habit-2.html.[95]

Frontiers. "Stressed? Take a 20-Minute 'Nature Pill'." *ScienceDaily*, 4 Apr. 2019,
www.sciencedaily.com/releases/2019/04/190404074915.htm.[144]

Gallagher, Matthew W., and Shane J. Lopez. "Positive Expectancies and Mental
Health: Identifying the Unique Contributions of Hope and Optimism."
Taylor & Francis, Informa UK Limited, 5 Nov. 2009,
www.tandfonline.com/doi/abs/10.1080/17439760903157166?journalCo
de=rpos20&%C2%A0.[22]

Garcia-Hill, E. "Reticular Activating System." *Science Direct*, Elsevier, 2009,
www.sciencedirect.com/topics/neuroscience/reticular-activating-system.[24]

Gillihan, Seth J. "How Helping Others Can Relieve Anxiety and Depression."
Psychology Today, Sussex Publishers, 10 Oct. 2017,
www.psychologytoday.com/us/blog/think-act-be/201710/how-helping-
others-can-relieve-anxiety-and-depression. [68, 69]

Gino, Francesca. "Are You Too Stressed to Be Productive? Or Not Stressed
Enough?" *Harvard Business Review*, Harvard University, 14 Apr. 2016,

hbr.org/2016/04/are-you-too-stressed-to-be-productive-or-not-stressed-enough.[87]

Goodreads. "John Gardner (Author of Grendel)." *Goodreads*, 2020, www.goodreads.com/author/show/481146.John_Gardner.[179]

Grady, Cheryl L., et al. "Neural Correlates of the Episodic Encoding of Pictures and Words." *PNAS*, National Academy of Sciences, 3 Mar. 1998, www.pnas.org/content/95/5/2703.[83]

Grohol, John M. "Depression: Symptoms, Types & Treatments." *Psych Central*, 28 Apr. 2020, psychcentral.com/disorders/depression/.[85, 86]

Groth, Aimee. "If You Want to Be Happy, Stop Comparing Yourself to Others." *Business Insider*, 21 Apr. 2013, www.businessinsider.com/happiness-research-2013-4.[163]

Gruber, June. "The Myth of Good and Bad Emotions." *Science & Nonduality*, SAND, 2020, www.scienceandnonduality.com/article/sadness-is-always-bad-happiness-is-always-good.[5, 167]

Gustafson, Craig. "Bruce Lipton, PhD: The Jump From Cell Culture to Consciousness." *National Center for Biotechnology Information*, US National Library of Medicine, Dec. 2017, www.ncbi.nlm.nih.gov/pmc/articles/PMC6438088/.[26]

Hall-Flavin, Daniel K. "Vitamin B-12 and Depression: Are They Related?" *Mayo Clinic*, Mayo Foundation for Medical Education and Research, 1 June 2018, www.mayoclinic.org/diseases-conditions/depression/expert-answers/vitamin-b12-and-depression/faq-20058077.[77]

Harbinger, Jordan. "Why You Compare Yourself to Other People (And How to Stop)." *Jordan Harbinger*, 26 Mar. 2018, www.jordanharbinger.com/why-you-compare-yourself-to-other-people-and-how-to-stop-2/.[161, 162, 164]

Harvard Health Publishing. "Exercising to Relax." *Harvard Health*, Harvard University, 13 July 2018, www.health.harvard.edu/staying-healthy/exercising-to-relax.[47, 140, 169]

Harvard Health Publishing. "Sour Mood Getting You down? Get Back to
Nature." *Harvard Medical School*, Harvard University, July 2018,
www.health.harvard.edu/mind-and-mood/sour-mood-getting-you-down-
get-back-to-nature.[45]

Hedaya, Robert J. "Vitamin B12." *Psychology Today*, Sussex Publishers, 2 Feb.
2012, www.psychologytoday.com/us/blog/health-
matters/201202/vitamin-b12.[72]

Help Guide. "Laughter Is the Best Medicine." *HelpGuide.org*, 16 Apr. 2020,
www.helpguide.org/articles/mental-health/laughter-is-the-best-
medicine.htm.[56, 181]

Horn, Stacy. "Singing Changes Your Brain." *Time*, Time USA, LLC, 16 Aug.
2013, ideas.time.com/2013/08/16/singing-changes-your-brain/.[32]

Humes, Jimmy. "What Are the Health Benefits of Humor and Laughter?"
Expand Project, 21 Apr. 2019, www.expandproject.eu/what-are-the-
health-benefits-of-humor-and-laughter.[57]

Huntley, Robyn. "What Is Cognitive Behavior Therapy (CBT)." *PrairieCare*, 22
Aug. 2014, www.prairie-care.com/blog/what-is-cognitive-behavior-
therapy-cbt-by-robyn-huntley-lmft/.[153]

Hyman, Ira E. "Worrying about Money." *Psychology Today*, Sussex Publishers, 11
Jan. 2019, www.psychologytoday.com/us/blog/mental-
mishaps/201901/worrying-about-money.[216]

Ibrahim, Banu. "Stressed at Work? A Zen Garden Might Be the Answer to
Helping You Relax." *CNN*, Cable News Network, 8 Aug. 2018,
www.cnn.com/2018/08/08/cnn-underscored/zen-garden-sand-
shop/index.html.[149]

James, Matt. "8 Beliefs You Should Have About Money." *Psychology Today*,
Sussex Publishers, 6 Apr. 2016, www.psychologytoday.com/us/blog/focus-
forgiveness/201604/8-beliefs-you-should-have-about-money.[213]

Kennedy, David O. "B Vitamins and the Brain: Mechanisms, Dose and Efficacy-
-A Review." *National Center for Biotechnology Information*, US National

Library of Medicine, 27 Jan. 2016,
www.ncbi.nlm.nih.gov/pmc/articles/PMC4772032/.[76]

Khan, Kauser. "How Somatic Therapy Can Help Patients Suffering from
Psychological Trauma." *Psych Central*, 8 July 2018,
psychcentral.com/blog/how-somatic-therapy-can-help-patients-suffering-
from-psychological-trauma/.[19]

Killgore, William D.S. "Effects of Sleep Deprivation on Cognition." *Progress in
Brain Research*, Elsevier, 12 Nov. 2010,
www.sciencedirect.com/science/article/pii/B9780444537027000075.[100]

Kind, Shelley, and Stefan G. Hofmann. "Facts about the Effects of Mindfulness."
Anxiety.org, 10 Feb. 2016, www.anxiety.org/can-mindfulness-help-reduce-
anxiety.[147]

Kindt, Merel. "The Memrec Method." *Kindt Clinics*, 2020,
kindtclinics.com/en/treatment/%C2%A0%C2%A0%C2%A0.[136]

LaMonte, Wayne W. "The Theory of Planned Behavior." *Boston University School
of Public Health*, 9 Sept. 2019, sphweb.bumc.bu.edu/otlt/MPH-
Modules/SB/BehavioralChangeTheories/BehavioralChangeTheories3.html.[23]

Layton, Julia. "Does Singing Make You Happy?" *HowStuffWorks Science*,
HowStuffWorks, 27 Jan. 2020, science.howstuffworks.com/life/inside-
the-mind/emotions/singing-happy1.htm.[34]

Leonard, Jayne. "REM Sleep: Definition, Functions, the Effects of Alcohol, and
Disorders." *Medical News Today*, MediLexicon International, 1 Sept.
2017, www.medicalnewstoday.com/articles/247927.[103]

Mann, Denise. "Even Mild Dehydration May Cause Emotional, Physical
Problems." *WebMD*, WebMD, 20 Jan. 2012,
www.webmd.com/women/news/20120120/even-mild-dehydration-may-
cause-emotional-physical-problems#1.[71]

Marciniak, Martin D, et al. "The Cost of Treating Anxiety: the Medical and
Demographic Correlates That Impact Total Medical Costs." *National
Center for Biotechnology Information*, U.S. National Library of Medicine,
2005, www.ncbi.nlm.nih.gov/pubmed/16075454%C2%A0.[15]

Mawer, Rudy. "17 Proven Tips to Sleep Better." *Healthline*, 27 Feb. 2020, www.healthline.com/nutrition/17-tips-to-sleep-better. [48, 141]

Mayo Clinic. "Exercise and Stress: Get Moving to Manage Stress." *Mayo Clinic*, Mayo Foundation for Medical Education and Research, 8 Mar. 2018, www.mayoclinic.org/healthy-lifestyle/stress-management/in-depth/exercise-and-stress/art-20044469 [46, 138]

McCraty, R, et al. "The Impact of a New Emotional Self-Management Program on Stress, Emotions, Heart Rate Variability, DHEA and Cortisol." *Integrative Physiological and Behavioral Science: the Official Journal of the Pavlovian Society*, U.S. National Library of Medicine, 1998, www.ncbi.nlm.nih.gov/pubmed/9737736%C2%A0. [187]

McCulligh, Chantal. "Gratitude and Anxiety: 8 Ways Gratitude Can Help Anxiety Sufferers." *8 Ways Gratitude Can Help Anxiety Sufferers*, 26 June 2019, anxiety-gone.com/8-ways-gratitude-can-help-anxiety-sufferers/. [188, 192]

McCulligh, Chantal. "Studies Reveal You Can Rewire Your Brain with Neuroplasticity for Anxiety." *Anxiety Gone*, 26 June 2019, anxiety-gone.com/studies-reveal-you-can-rewire-your-brain-with-neuroplasticity-for-anxiety/%C2%A0. [191]

McCulligh, Chantal. "Top 9 Methods for Beating Social Anxiety." *Anxiety Gone*, 28 Oct. 2019, anxiety-gone.com/top-9-methods-for-beating-social-anxiety/%C2%A0. [185]

McPherson, Fiona. "The Role of Emotion in Memory." *About Memory*, 18 Nov. 2011, www.memory-key.com/memory/emotion. [130]

Mental Health America. "Connect with Others." *Mental Health America*, Mental Health America Inc., 2020, www.mhanational.org/connect-others. [59]

Mental Health America. "Create Joy and Satisfaction." *Mental Health America*, 2020, www.mhanational.org/create-joy-and-satisfaction. [183]

Merriam-Webster. "Fear." *Merriam-Webster*, Merriam-Webster, 2020, www.merriam-webster.com/dictionary/fear. [1]

Merriam-Webster. "Intrinsic." *Merriam-Webster*, 2020, www.merriam-webster.com/dictionary/intrinsic.[173]

Merriam-Webster. "Panic." *Merriam-Webster*, Merriam-Webster, 2020, www.merriam-webster.com/dictionary/panic.[2]

Merriam-Webster. "Worry." *Merriam-Webster*, Merriam-Webster, 2020, www.merriam-webster.com/dictionary/worry.[3]

Miller, Greg. "How Our Brains Make Memories." *Smithsonian.com*, Smithsonian Institution, 1 May 2010, www.smithsonianmag.com/science-nature/how-our-brains-make-memories-14466850/.[128]

Moyer, Nancy, and Timothy J. Legg. "Amygdala Hijack: When Emotion Takes Over." *Healthline*, Healthline, 22 Apr. 2109, www.healthline.com/health/stress/amygdala-hijack#takeaway.[7]

Multivitamin Guide. "The Multivitamin Guide." *MultivitaminGuide.org*, 2020, www.multivitaminguide.org/.[78]

National Institute of Neurological Disorders and Stroke. "Brain Basics: Understanding Sleep." *National Institute of Neurological Disorders and Stroke*, U.S. Department of Health and Human Services, 13 Aug. 2019, www.ninds.nih.gov/disorders/Patient-Caregiver-Education/Understanding-Sleep.[97, 101, 107]

National Sleep Foundation. "How to Design a Nighttime Routine." *Sleep.org*, 2020, www.sleep.org/articles/design-perfect-bedtime-routine/.[122]

National Sleep Foundation. "The Truth About Whether Your Dreams Affect the Quality of Your Sleep." *National Sleep Foundation*, 2020, www.sleepfoundation.org/articles/do-dreams-affect-how-well-you-sleep.[104]

National Sleep Foundation. "What to Do When You Wake up in the Middle of the Night." *Sleep.org*, 2020, www.sleep.org/articles/tips-wake-middle-night/.[123]

Newport Academy. "10 Ways Pets and Mental Health Go Together." *Newport Academy*, 4 June 2018, www.newportacademy.com/resources/well-being/pets-and-mental-health/.[151]

Occidental Asset Management, LLC. "Find Out Your Money Script!" *Occidental Asset Management, LLC*, 2020, www.yourmentalwealthadvisors.com/find-out-your-money-script. [209, 210, 211, 212]

Orloff, Judith. "5 Protection Techniques for Sensitive People." *Psychology Today*, Sussex Publishers, 19 Apr. 2018, www.psychologytoday.com/us/blog/the-empaths-survival-guide/201804/5-protection-techniques-sensitive-people. [51]

PBS News Hour. "Can Trauma Be Passed to next Generation through DNA?" *PBS*, Public Broadcasting Service, 2015, www.pbs.org/newshour/extra/daily-videos/can-trauma-be-passed-to-next-generation-through-dna/. [131]

Peters, Brandon. "Reticular Activating System and Your Sleep." *Very Well Health*, 1 Sept. 2019, www.verywellhealth.com/definition-of-reticular-activating-system-3015376#citation-1. [115]

Physicians' Diagnostic & Rehabilitation. "Benefits of Abdominal Breathing Techniques." *PDR Clinics*, Physicians' Diagnostic & Rehabilitation, 23 Apr. 2019, pdrclinics.com/2014/11/breathing-benefits/. [96]

Popova, Maria. "How Repetition Enchants the Brain and the Psychology of Why We Love It in Music." *Brain Pickings*, 14 Feb. 2016, www.brainpickings.org/2014/09/18/on-repeat-margulis/. [61, 62, 64]

Popova, Maria. "The Backfire Effect: The Psychology of Why We Have a Hard Time Changing Our Minds." *Brain Pickings*, 21 Sept. 2016, www.brainpickings.org/2014/05/13/backfire-effect-mcraney/. [30, 63]

Popova, Maria. "Viktor Frankl on the Human Search for Meaning." *Brain Pickings*, 5 Feb. 2017, www.brainpickings.org/2013/03/26/viktor-frankl-mans-search-for-meaning/. [175]

Premack, Rachel. "17 Seriously Disturbing Facts about Your Job." *Business Insider*, Business Insider, 2 Aug. 2018, www.businessinsider.com/disturbing-facts-about-your-job-2011-2. [203]

Psychologist World. "Emotion and Memory: How Do Your Emotions Affect Your Ability To Remember Information And Recall Past Memories?" *Psychologist World*, 23 Feb. 2016, www.psychologistworld.com/emotion/emotion-memory-psychology.[126]

Psychologist World. "Emotions and Memory." *Psychologist World*, 2020, www.psychologistworld.com/emotion/emotion-memory-psychology.[202]

Psychology Today. "Cognitive Behavioral Therapy." *Psychology Today*, Sussex Publishers, 2020, www.psychologytoday.com/us/basics/cognitive-behavioral-therapy.[21]

Psychology Today. "Depression." *Psychology Today*, Sussex Publishers Inc., 2020, www.psychologytoday.com/us/basics/depression.[74]

Psychology Today. "Social Comparison Theory." *Psychology Today*, Sussex Publishers, 2020, www.psychologytoday.com/us/basics/social-comparison-theory.[159]

Ramakrishnan, Kalyanakrishnan, and Dewey C. Scheid. "Treatment Options for Insomnia." *American Family Physician*, 15 Aug. 2007, www.aafp.org/afp/2007/0815/p517.html.[111]

Reh, F. John. "Why You Should Try Chunking to Increase Your Work Efficiency." *The Balance Careers*, The Balance Careers, 4 July 2019, www.thebalancecareers.com/dont-multi-task-when-you-can-use-chunking-2276184.[207]

Robbins, Mel. "The Five Elements of the 5 Second Rule." *Mel Robbins*, 8 Oct. 2019, melrobbins.com/five-elements-5-second-rule/.[35]

Robinson, Kara Mayer. "How Pets Help Manage Depression." *WebMD*, WebMD, 4 Dec. 2017, www.webmd.com/depression/features/pets-depression#1.[65, 150]

Sampson, Hannah. "What Does America Have against Vacation?" *The Washington Post*, WP Company, 28 Aug. 2019, www.washingtonpost.com/travel/2019/08/28/what-does-america-have-against-vacation/.[208]

Sauter, Steven, et al. "Stress at Work." *CDC*, U.S. Department of Health and Human Services, 1999, www.cdc.gov/niosh/docs/99-101/pdfs/99-101.pdf?id=10.26616/NIOSHPUB99101.[205]

Science Learning Hub. "Colours of Light." *Science Learning Hub*, 2020, www.sciencelearn.org.nz/resources/47-colours-of-light.[120]

Science of People. "The Benefits of Music: How the Science of Music Can Help You." *Science of People*, 22 Apr. 2020, www.scienceofpeople.com/benefits-music/.[90]

Scott, Elizabeth. "Journaling Is a Great Tool for Coping with Anxiety." *Verywell Mind*, 26 Jan. 2020, www.verywellmind.com/journaling-a-great-tool-for-coping-with-anxiety-3144672.[124]

Scott, Elizabeth. "What Is the Relaxation Response?" *Very Well Mind*, 12 Mar. 2020, www.verywellmind.com/what-is-the-relaxation-response-3145145.[98]

Selby, Edward A. "Rumination: Problem Solving Gone Wrong." *Psychology Today*, Sussex Publishers, 24 Feb. 2010, www.psychologytoday.com/us/blog/overcoming-self-sabotage/201002/rumination-problem-solving-gone-wrong.[52]

Selhub, Eva. "Nutritional Psychiatry: Your Brain on Food." *Harvard Medical School*, Harvard University, 31 Mar. 2020, www.health.harvard.edu/blog/nutritional-psychiatry-your-brain-on-food-201511168626.[70]

Selva, Joaquin. "Logotherapy: Viktor Frankl's Theory of Meaning." *PositivePsychology.com*, 27 Oct. 2019, positivepsychology.com/viktor-frankl-logotherapy/.[176]

Semeco, Arlene. "How to Start Exercising: A Beginner's Guide to Working Out." *Healthline*, 2 Mar. 2017, www.healthline.com/nutrition/how-to-start-exercising.[143]

Shiel, William C. "Definition of Stress." *MedicineNet*, MedicineNet, 11 Dec. 2018, www.medicinenet.com/script/main/art.asp?articlekey=20104.[4]

Shrestha, Praveen. "Yerkes - Dodson Law." *Psychestudy*, Psychestudy, 17 Nov. 2017, www.psychestudy.com/general/motivation-emotion/yerkes-dodson-law%C2%A0.[13]

Sicinski, Adam. "10 Cognitive Distortions That Are Sabotaging Your Brain." *IQ Doodle*, 18 Sept. 2019, iqdoodle.com/cognitive-distortions/.[154]

Slide, Casey. "How to Stop Worrying About Money." *Money Crashers*, 2020, www.moneycrashers.com/stop-worrying-money/.[215]

Social Psych Online. "The Mere Exposure Effect." *Social Psych Online*, 5 Mar. 2016, socialpsychonline.com/2016/03/the-mere-exposure-effect/.[29]

Sollitto, Marlo. "Sick with Worry: How Thoughts Affect Your Health." *Aging Care*, 11 Nov. 2010, www.agingcare.com/articles/health-problems-caused-by-stress-143376.htm.[18]

Stevens, Suzanne. "Chapter 2 - Sleep and Wakefulness." *Textbook of Clinical Neurology*, edited by Wayne A. Hening, (Third Edition) ed., Elsevier Inc, 2007, pp. 21–33.[88]

Stibich, Mark. "Why Do People Dream During the REM Stage of Sleep?" *Verywell Mind*, Verywell Mind, 5 Feb. 2020, www.verywellmind.com/understanding-dreams-2224258.[105]

Stollings, Linda. "Withholding Forgiveness Can Be Toxic To Your Health." *Bristol Herald Courier*, 4 Oct. 2016, www.heraldcourier.com/lifestyles/withholding-forgiveness-can-be-toxic-to-your-health/article_7b25c7de-8a64-11e6-b107-7fdbac433602.html.[195]

Storoni, Mithu. "Nature Is Calming -- Even If It Isn't Real." *Psychology Today*, Sussex Publishers, 31 Dec. 2018, www.psychologytoday.com/us/blog/the-stress-proof-life/201812/nature-is-calming-even-if-it-isnt-real.[148]

Tapia, Jesus A., et al. "Reticular Activating System of a Central Pattern Generator: Premovement Electrical Potentials." *The Physiological Society*, 24 Oct. 2013, physoc.onlinelibrary.wiley.com/doi/full/10.1002/phy2.129.[114]

Tateo, Luca. "Just an Illusion? Imagination as Higher Mental Function." *Semantic Scholar*, 1 Jan. 1970, www.semanticscholar.org/paper/Just-an-Illusion-Imagination-as-Higher-Mental-Tateo/cbc7de68c7916fae099f08a33f52312dd8704c7f. [91, 92]

Ten Boom, Corrie. "Guideposts Classics: Corrie Ten Boom on Forgiveness." *Guideposts*, 24 July 2014, www.guideposts.org/better-living/positive-living/guideposts-classics-corrie-ten-boom-on-forgiveness. [200, 201]

Ten Boom, Corrie. *The Hiding Place*. Chosen Books, 1999. [199]

The American Institute of Stress. "Workplace Stress." *The American Institute of Stress*, 20 Feb. 2020, www.stress.org/workplace-stress. [204]

The Brain from Top to Bottom. "Tool Module: Human Memory versus Computer Memory." *Tool Module: Primatology*, 2020, thebrain.mcgill.ca/flash/capsules/outil_bleu05.html. [129]

Thoma, Myriam V, et al. "The Effect of Music on the Human Stress Response." *PloS One*, Public Library of Science, 5 Aug. 2013, www.ncbi.nlm.nih.gov/pmc/articles/PMC3734071/%C2%A0. [84]

Thum, Myrko. "The 10 Most Limiting Beliefs About Money (& How to Remove Them)." *Myrko Thum*, 21 June 2013, www.myrkothum.com/limiting-beliefs-about-money/. [214]

Toepfer, Steven M., et al. "Letters of Gratitude: Further Evidence for Author Benefits." *Research Gate*, Mar. 2012, www.researchgate.net/publication/225805768_Letters_of_Gratitude_Further_Evidence_for_Author_Benefits. [186]

University of Amsterdam. "Professor Merel Kindt." *University of Amsterdam*, 2 Jan. 2020, www.uva.nl/en/profile/k/i/m.kindt/m.kindt.html. [133]

University of British Columbia. "Sit, Stay, Heal: Study Finds Therapy Dogs Help Stressed University Students." *ScienceDaily*, 12 Mar. 2018, www.sciencedaily.com/releases/2018/03/180312085045.htm. [66]

University of East Anglia. "It's Official -- Spending Time Outside Is Good for You." *ScienceDaily*, 6 July 2018, www.sciencedaily.com/releases/2018/07/180706102842.htm.[43, 145]

University of Florida. "Why Debt Destroys Marriages and How to Fight Back." *Why Debt Destroys Marriages and How to Fight Back - SMART Couples - University of Florida, Institute of Food and Agricultural Sciences - UF/IFAS*, University of Florida, Institute of Food and Agricultural Sciences, 2020, smartcouples.ifas.ufl.edu/engaged/marriage-basics/why-debt-destroys-marriages-and-how-to-fight-back/.[218]

University of Groningen. "Music Changes Perception, Research Shows." *ScienceDaily*, 27 Apr. 2011, www.sciencedaily.com/releases/2011/04/110427101606.htm.[89]

University of Minnesota. "How Does Nature Impact Our Wellbeing?" *Taking Charge of Your Health & Wellbeing*, University of Minnesota, 2016, www.takingcharge.csh.umn.edu/how-does-nature-impact-our-wellbeing.[44, 146]

University of Rochester Medical Center. "Journaling for Mental Health." *Journaling for Mental Health - Health Encyclopedia - University of Rochester Medical Center*, University of Rochester Medical Center , 2020, www.urmc.rochester.edu/encyclopedia/content.aspx?ContentID=4552&ContentTypeID=1.[125]

University of Tennessee at Knoxville. "Psychologists Find Smiling Really Can Make People Happier." *ScienceDaily*, 12 Apr. 2019, www.sciencedaily.com/releases/2019/04/190412094728.htm.[39]

Vaisman, Boris. "Negative Social Comparison Affecting Mental Health." *Seasons in Malibu*, 2 July 2019, seasonsmalibu.com/negative-social-comparison-affecting-mental-health/.[166]

Vishton, Peter M. *Outsmart Yourself: Brain-Based Strategies to a Better You*. The Teaching Company, 2016.[108, 109, 110, 113, 118, 127]

Weil, Andrew. "What Is Guided Imagery?" *DrWeil.com*, Healthy Lifestyle Brands, LLC., 20 June 2019, www.drweil.com/health-wellness/balanced-living/wellness-therapies/guided-imagery-therapy/%C2%A0.[168]

Wenner, Melinda. "Smile! It Could Make You Happier!" *Scientific American*,
Springer Nature America, Inc., 1 Sept. 2009,
www.scientificamerican.com/article/smile-it-could-make-you-happier/. [37, 41]

William & Mary. "Peter Vishton Associate Professor of Psychological Sciences."
William & Mary, 2020,
www.wm.edu/as/neuroscience/faculty/vishton_p.php. [117]

Winch, Guy. "10 Surprising Reasons You Shouldn't Brood." *Psychology Today*,
Sussex Publishers, 15 Feb. 2015, www.psychologytoday.com/us/blog/the-
squeaky-wheel/201502/10-surprising-reasons-you-shouldnt-brood. [53]

Winch, Guy. "Why We All Need to Practice Emotional First Aid." *TED*,
TEDxLinnaeusUniversity, Nov. 2014,
www.ted.com/talks/guy_winch_why_we_all_need_to_practice_emotional
_first_aid?referrer=playlist-the_importance_of_self_care. [55, 60]

Wong, Joel, and Joshua Brown. "How Gratitude Changes You and Your Brain."
Greater Good Magazine, Berkeley University of California, 6 June 2017,
greatergood.berkeley.edu/article/item/how_gratitude_changes_you_and_y
our_brain. [189, 190]

Zisapel, Nava. "New Perspectives on the Role of Melatonin in Human Sleep,
Circadian Rhythms and Their Regulation." *British Journal of
Pharmacology*, John Wiley and Sons Inc., Aug. 2018,
www.ncbi.nlm.nih.gov/pmc/articles/PMC6057895/. [119]

APPENDIX G

OTHER WORKS BY LINDA BJORK

Lindabjorkauthor.com

Crushed, A Journey Through Depression

An inspiring true story of triumph over despair so relatable and unflinchingly honest that you'll wonder if you're reading your own story, and will start believing in your own happy ending. This captivating narrative empowers the reader with tools to revive hope and facilitate healing. Here's what readers are saying:

I couldn't put it down! I loved how the author showed greatness through trial and tribulation, and how real and raw her emotions were throughout the book. I laughed, I cried, and I celebrated as she conquered life throughout her journey! This book was life changing, deepening my vision as to how we can truly learn and become better from other's experiences! Everyone who reads it will find some way that they can relate to the author's experiences and at the same time gain insight as to how to cope with the struggles of life! Such an amazing read! One that I will read over and over again!!!

-Misty C.

A very personal, honest, and insightful journey of self-reflection and emotional healing. We are all broken to some degree and need to be aware of some of the tools we have to find healing and mending the things that create a false and negative self-image. Linda has opened herself up in a very vulnerable way to allow you on that journey of healing in the hopes that you may find something of value in there to help with your healing. I did, and I hope you will as well.

-Troy J.

I couldn't put this book down. Linda is so real, so honest, and made it easy for me to identify things in my own life that I needed to process and let go of. She clearly explains her entire journey, from a lifetime of being depressed and suicidal to finding contentment and self-love.

-Jane D.

Heartbreakingly resonant for every invisible woman. A beautifully written display of how generational pain can lead to generational healing.

-Sherrie C.

Bjork takes readers through some very personal and real struggles and points them to the light at the end of the dark tunnel of depression. She provides readers with resources that allow them to emerge from that tunnel and embrace new levels of happiness.

-Debbie E.

It's a great read! I was hooked from the start and read it in one sitting! I am so happy Linda chose to share her personal journey from such inner turmoil to finding hope and joy in life once more! It makes me wonder how many others may have similar false beliefs about themselves that are holding them back from the joy this life is meant to be. How grateful I am that she was courageous enough to face her struggles and challenge them! She is so open and descriptive of the healing process she took that anyone can benefit from her story.

-Lindsay S.

Linda is an amazing writer and has done a superb job with this book of self-exploration and mastery over a difficult and debilitating subject. Great and satisfying read.

-Marie R.

I had a hard time putting it down. This book caused me to think differently about others, and the secret pain that so many carry. But, by far the greater portion of this book is about the process of healing that took the author from crushed to truly recovering, and in the process healing many of her relationships as well. My favorite thing about this book is the detail it gives of the various tools she learned for recovery. It has caused me to think differently in ways that are affecting my own happiness. There are many people I know who I hope will read this book and be blessed by it.

-David C.

30 Days to Alleviate Depression: Backed by Science. Verified by Experience.

This book is available to download for free on the Hope for Healing website. Please visit hopeforhealingfoundation.org to learn more. *30 Days to Alleviate Depression* is an easy-to-follow guidebook to help alleviate symptoms of depression. Complete, step by step coaching guides you through each day explaining not only what to do, but why it works. Happiness is available just around the corner, start on the pathway today! Here's what readers are saying:

Linda gives true principles that can lift and bring joy. My heart and mind were touched by Linda's work. I like the clearness and simplicity of her writing. She has experienced first-hand what she presents and teaches. Her principles are organized into a step-by-step guidebook that have helped me in learning how to cope and grow. She has researched and presents verified information about why it worked. My experience in reading and studying these ideas has been uplifting and helped me move forward. I highly recommend it!

-M. Grover

Real help! Linda has been down the path of depression and successfully pulled herself out with the help of simple tools that really work. A great book for those wanting a happier, more hopeful life

-S. Lindsay

30 Days to a Better Marriage

This book is available to download for free on the Hope for Healing website. Please visit hopeforhealingfoundation.org to learn more. Everybody knows that a marriage can deteriorate, but not everybody knows that a marriage can be rejuvenated. This step by step guidebook includes a comprehensive plan with simple daily action steps that can change your relationship and your life! Whatever the current condition of your marriage, following the principles in this book will improve it even more.

Pathway to Happiness

This book is available to download for free on the Hope for Healing website. Please visit hopeforhealingfoundation.org to learn more. *Pathway to Happiness* contains a flexible outline where you create your own wellness goals and choose from a wide selection of wellness tools to suit your particular needs. It is a simple step-by-step action plan to awaken the answers that are already inside of you.

Hope for Healing (hopeforhealingfoundation.org)

Linda Bjork is the founder and executive director of Hope for Healing non-profit charity. We can all use a little more peace and happiness in our lives. Hope for Healing offers tools, information, resources, and a plan to increase happiness, build confidence and self-esteem, strengthen families and marriages, manage stress, and help alleviate symptoms of depression and anxiety. You have more power than you might think.

Two Good Things (twogoodthings.net)

Two Good Things is the Bjork family blog. At our house we eat dinner together as a family, and everyone takes turns sharing two good things about their day. This simple tradition helps us stay connected. Two Good Things is about a normal family doing normal things, which in today's day and age is rather abnormal. We have a variety of interests including: food, family, aviation, art, travel, do-it-yourself projects, homeschooling, mommy blog, and more.

Innovative Joy LLC (innovativejoy.com)

Linda Bjork is the owner of Innovative Joy LLC. We help people become their best selves. A great resource to find Linda's books and courses.

Linda's Corner: Faith, Family, and Living Joyfully

Linda's Corner podcast was created to inspire hope, increase joy, and motivate positive change by talking about things that really matter. We'll discuss topics like: family and relationships; increasing happiness; physical, mental and emotional health; self-improvement; and building your faith so that it's bigger than your fears. Available on Apple Podcasts and Spotify.

.

Made in the USA
Coppell, TX
16 January 2023

11209417R10164